AND THEN THE END WILL COME!
(but five things you need to know in the meantime)

Brandon Andress

authorHOUSE®

AuthorHouse™
1663 Liberty Drive
Bloomington, IN 47403
www.authorhouse.com
Phone: 1-800-839-8640

Published by AuthorHouse 4/1/2013

ISBN: 978-1-4817-3563-6 (sc)
ISBN: 978-1-4817-3562-9 (hc)
ISBN: 978-1-4817-3561-2 (e)

Library of Congress Control Number: 2013905817

This book is printed on acid-free paper.

This book is dedicated to my beautiful family.
Jenny, Anna, Caroline, and Will
each of you have taught me how to be
more like Christ each day, making me a
better husband and a better dad.

*This work is made possible through the love
and support of some amazing people in my
life to whom I am eternally grateful
Peace, Blessings, and Love to...*

*Mike and Jodi Engelstad
Steve and Karlyn Bellinger
David and Shannan Fields*

I would like to thank some very close friends who gave their time and experience and talents to make this work a reality
Whitney Ulm- Eminence Photography
Andy J. Miller- Design KOMA
Erica Sahm- Editor extraordinaire
Herb Haile- The Reality Check Man

MATTHEW 24: 1-14

Jesus departed from the temple area and was going on his way when his disciples came up to him to call his attention to the buildings of the temple *and* point them out to him.

But he answered them. Do you see all these? Truly I tell you, there will not be left here one stone upon another that will not be thrown down.

While he was seated on the Mount of Olives, the disciples came to him privately and said, tell us, when will this take place, and what will be the sign of your coming and of the End (the completion, the consummation) of the Age?

Jesus answered them, be careful that no one misleads you [deceiving you and leading you into error].

For many will come in (on the strength of) my name appropriating the name which belongs to me, saying, I am the Christ (the Messiah), and they will lead many astray.

And you will hear of wars and rumors of wars; see that you are not frightened *or* troubled, for this must take place, but the end is not yet.

For nation will rise against nation, and kingdom against kingdom, and there will be famines and earthquakes in place after place.

All this is but the beginning [the early pains] of the birth pangs [of the intolerable anguish].

Then they will hand you over to suffer affliction *and* tribulation and put you to death, and you will be hated by all nations for my name's sake.

And then many will be offended *and* repelled *and* will begin to distrust *and* desert [him whom they ought to trust and obey] *and* will stumble and fall away and betray one another *and* pursue one another with hatred.

And many false prophets will rise up and deceive *and* lead many into error.

And the love of the great body of people will grow cold because of the multiplied lawlessness *and* iniquity, but he who endures to the end will be saved.

And this good news of the kingdom (the Gospel) will be preached throughout the whole world as a testimony to all the nations, and then will come the end.

TABLE OF CONTENTS

INTRODUCTION!

AND THEN THE END WILL COME!

Got your attention, didn't I?

You have to admit that it is really a brilliant idea.

You know, saying something about the "End Times."

It always gets a huge buzz going.

And it attracts tons of attention and sells millions of books, right?

I think so.

And maybe that is the genius of titling this book *And Then The End Will Come*!

Everyone wants to know the *when's* and *what's* of how this thing is gonna go down.

Some maybe more than others, but it doesn't take much to attract a curious crowd.

It is like that old trick where a couple of people begin looking into the air pretending that they see something interesting. They stand there captivated looking into the air, curiously stroking their chins, but utterly looking at nothing.

And before you know it one person stops, and then another, and then another until there is a large group of people congregating and looking up into the air at the spectacular sight of... absolutely nothing.

And that is the fascinating thing about human beings – *our curiosity is a strange attractor.*

Have you ever been in a traffic jam on the interstate?

And then, after five hours of creeping at two miles per hour in the southbound lane, you find out that the accident that caused the traffic jam is, in fact, not even going southbound!

The accident was in the northbound lane!

So the southbound travelers in front of me, well, they were rubbernecking.

And rubbernecking, in my book, is curiosity.

Incidents such as these reveal an all-important reality – we have a deep desire to be in on *the thing*.

Whatever that *thing* happens to be.

And it hardly ever matters what that *thing* is.

We want access to insider information.

Especially if it is mysterious or out of the ordinary!

So when it comes to matters of the "End Times," we search for someone or something that will tell us definitively how it will all shake out.

Our curiosity demands it.

We seek after those who seem to have an insider's take on what to expect, how to prepare, and what to buy.

We are especially drawn to those who seem to have special insight into deciphering the symbols and language of esoteric and ancient texts.

And we consume books and movies that bring all of it to life.

_____

How do I know?

I won't mention any names, but you know those bestselling books and movies that talk about how if we don't believe that *heaven is for real* then we might be *left behind* on this *late, great planet earth*.

I say that tongue in cheek, of course.

But seriously... I only say it that way to illustrate just how mainstream our curiosity is when it comes to the supernatural, to life-after-death, and especially the "End Times."

Millions of dollars are spent each year buying books and watching movies explaining another "unique perspective" as to how it will all end or what we can expect on the "other side."

More and more television shows are documenting the lives of people preparing for "Doomsday" and then showing the viewers how to prepare for the "End Times" themselves.

No joke.

And tons of people are tuning-in.

Did I mention that we are a curious and inquisitive people?

If there's a box, we want to know what's in it.
If there's a corner, we want to know what's around it.
If there's another dimension, we want to experience it.

Our inquiring minds want to know.
Our inquiring minds need to know.
Our inquiring minds HAVE TO KNOW!

And truth be told… I am not much different myself.

At 38-years-old I still can't wait to open my Christmas gifts.

I am either trying to sneak-a-peek weeks before they are wrapped – or – am guilty of not waiting my turn on Christmas morning.

Of course I am only halfway kidding, but you have to admit that you have, at least once, discretely ripped a bit of wrapping paper to take a sneak peek – or – flipped to the last page of a novel and read it before you had even read the middle two-thirds of the book.

So let's not act so self-righteous.

We are all guilty.

Are we not?

Of course I don't recommend skipping to the end of this book quite yet, because I haven't even had a chance to make my first point.

The underlying reality is that we all want to know about those things that are just out of our reach.

It's as if wanting to know the end, or that which is veiled, or that which is hidden from view is somehow wrapped up in our DNA.

Maybe it's just how we are made.

We want to know how the story ends.

_____

And it makes perfect sense.

We are story-people who are drawn to the story.

Protagonists.
Antagonists.
Conflict.
Resolution.

Stories pull us in because we identify so closely with them.

Whether we would admit it or not, or whether we are even aware of it or not, we are story-people because we are in our own story.

And our lives, like the stories we read, have protagonists and antagonists (and we have a choice as to who we would like to be).

Our lives, like the stories we read, are full of conflict on a daily basis and all throughout our lives that we either create or suffer through.

And in our lives, like the stories we read, we have a longing and a movement (surprise, surprise) toward an ending, toward a resolution.

So again, it makes sense – *we are hard-wired with a longing to know how it ends.*

We want to know how this conflict is fully resolved.

———

Which surprisingly doesn't make us much different than a handful of Jesus' curious disciples who wanted to know when they ought to expect his second coming at the End of the Age.

They too were interested in the *when* and the *what*.

Much like we are.

When are these things going to happen?

What will be the sign of Jesus' return?

Sound familiar?

I think we, too often, forget that the disciples where human beings just like us.

They had feelings.
They had ingrown toenails.
They had heartburn after eating at Miguel's.
They even got a little gassy from the frijoles.

Just like us.

And you can bet if we are inquisitive and curious, they were too.

But let's slow down and get some context first.

———

Jesus had just finished thrashing the religious leaders, the Pharisees.

6

And it was a serious thrashing.

A.
Serious.
Thrashing.

I know most people reference the "whipping" incident of Jesus clearing out the temple as his harshest moment.

But I would suggest reading the tongue-lashing, the verbal smack down (of course in love), that Jesus gave the religious leaders in Matthew 23.

Here is the basic flow of his tirade.

Hey Pharisees.
You are hopeless.
And frauds.
You are roadblocks.
And frauds.
You are ignorant.
And frauds.
Stupid Pharisees.
Oh yeah, and you are frauds.

Ouch.

What in the world set Jesus off like that?

The religious leaders had been so focused on the trivialities of life and nit-picking their way through it that they completely lost sight of living a full life with God presently.

They had lost sight of who they were supposed to be and what they were supposed to be doing as God's people in the present.

They had lost sight of their present identity and present purpose in their community and in the larger world.

7

So, in essence, they had lost sight of *right living, right now.*

Outward appearance had become more important than inward purity.

Hairsplitting oaths had become more important than honesty and integrity.

Nit-picking laws had become more important than fairness and compassion.

Religious tradition and ceremony had become more important than life-change.

And the disciples had been standing there listening to

Every.
Bit.
Of.
It.

So, of course, when Jesus had finally finished at the temple and they were making their way to the usual hangout, the Mount of Olives, the most obvious and pressing question from the disciples to Jesus was possibly, maybe something about...

The importance of not becoming too religious?

-or-

The importance of living a Godly life in the present?

Maybe it would have sounded something like this...

Hey Jesus... we want to make sure that we don't go down the same path as the religious leaders so what advice could you give us?

Hey Jesus... you know that thing you said to the religious leaders about being so obsessed with the Law of Moses that they missed being merciful and compassionate? Well, how do we balance following the law and being merciful and compassionate?

Hey Jesus, when you said that the religious leaders were dirty and corrupt on the inside while appearing to be clean and perfect on the outside, sometimes we feel that way. How do we make sure that we are clean on the inside?

Those would have been my good "Christianese" questions to Jesus had I been there.

And, of course with hindsight being 20/20, those are the types of questions I would have expected from the disciples immediately after they heard Jesus rail against the Pharisees.

But no.

Out of everything Jesus had just said to the Pharisees…

the one thing that got their attention…

the one thing they mentally filed away…

the one thing they set as a reminder in each of their iPhones…

was that small little blurb at the very end when Jesus mentioned that he would be leaving soon and that they wouldn't see him again until he returns!

———

And at that point, everything he said prior to that may as well have been forgotten.

Forget that 15-minute rant against the religious leaders.

Let's focus on the five-second snippet at the end!

It's like telling my kids a story about how important it is to be loving and kind and pure from the inside toward others... and then ending it by saying, "Treating others this way is as sweet as ice cream."

You *know* that they are going to focus on that sweet, creamy addition at the end!

But despite our unreasonably high expectations of what the disciples could have asked, they fell for Jesus' sweet bait.

And they were in full-on "End Times" and "Second Coming of Jesus" lock-down mode.

Can't you just hear them asking Jesus sheepishly...

(With a little throat clearing)

Ahem...Jesus...what was that last little tidbit you threw in there at the end?

You know...that business about your return?

We're kinda curious about that!

Please do share more.

I don't want you to take me the wrong way.

Curiosity isn't a bad thing at all.

Sure, it's a cat killer.

But beyond that... curiosity is an okay thing for humans.

And I think that Jesus thought it was an okay thing too.

Don't you find it interesting (and very telling) that after the disciples asked Jesus the *when* and *what* questions of his return... **he didn't punish them for their curiosity**?

There's no frustration.
There's no condemnation.
There's no belittling.
There's no rolling-of-the-eyes.
There's no dismissing them like they are kooks or weirdos.
There's no distancing from them as if they are an ideological fringe group.

There isn't any of that.

Not even a hint of it.

He simply takes the opportunity to reorient and reshape the entire discussion.

He reframes what's important in order to provide guidance moving forward.

And that is awesome.

It is so Jesus.

He doesn't make us feel ashamed or embarrassed when we are earnestly and curiously seeking and asking... even when our priorities are wrong.

He very simply and gently shows us what is really important.

Jesus understood, and still understands, our natural, God-given inclination toward *wanting to know, our longing for resolution, and our deep desire for heaven and earth to come gloriously together one day.*

———

The problem is when it starts to go beyond curiosity.

And then begins to affect our purpose on earth *right here, right now*.

That is when things can get really tricky and really off track.

Here we are… living and breathing… smack dab in the middle of our own story, and all of a sudden we become more preoccupied with trying to figure out how it ends than how we are going to live presently.

We become obsessed with the end before our story has even been developed, before the characters have even been fleshed out, before a movement toward resolution has even been set in motion.

So much so, we completely lose sight of the story itself.

We neglect the 150 pages in the middle.

We leave the plot unfinished.
We abandon the conflict.
We discard the character development.
We neglect our rhythm, our movement, our purpose.

We lose the beauty and the drama of our own narrative all the way up to, and culminating in, the climax and resolution.

We simply want to flip to the end of the book to see how it ends.

And that is where our minds stay…at the end.

And we wait.

Even though we are *here*.

Right now.

And that is what is so unfortunate, our *right here, right now* turns into nothing more than a waiting room.

And in the waiting room, people sit around and wait for someone to come for them.

I wonder if that is what Christ had in mind for our lives all along.

Waiting.

Where all we do is endure the hell around us.

Where all we do is pray fervently for him to "rescue us."

Sooner rather than later!

We get so fixated on the end that we begin missing what's in-between.

We get so fixated on the future that we miss the richness and opportunity of today.

Jesus, hurry up and come back so we don't have to deal with all of this world gone to hell-in-a-hand-basket.

Pronto.

But in the meantime, give us our $20 "End Times" fix and we will be waiting bags packed at the front door.

We promise.

Hallelujah.

_____

But here's the real dilemma as I see it.

If some Christians have been too zealous about the "End Times" and the "Second Coming of Christ"… there are other Christians who have swung way too far in the other direction.

To a place of "End Times" apathy.
To a place of "End Times" cynicism.
To a place of "End Times" skepticism.
To a place of "End Times" indifference.

While there was definitely a time when I would have planted myself squarely in the "End Times" and "Second Coming of Christ" hysteria camp… I have probably suffered from "Armageddon" fatigue and "Rapture" un-readiness for much of the last decade.

Do not take me the wrong way.

I am not saying that a pendulum swing far, far, far to the other side is a good move either.

Because I don't think it is.

If one extreme is over-zealousness to a fault then the other extreme is complete indifference and cynicism to a fault as well.

Many times with these big sweeping movements in one direction or the other… it's likely that the little baby Jesus gets thrown out with the bath water.

Technically, it would be the adult Jesus getting thrown out with the bath water… but that would have been too weird.

I digress.

My sharp pendulum swing movement in the opposite direction was likely more of a negative reaction to the over-zealousness of the entire "End Times" movement and how commercialized and sensationalized it had become… rather than the result of some scriptural epiphany.

And that's not a great thing either.

I just grew weary of the mania every time there was another war in the world, or another earthquake, or another news report of someone trying to broker an Israeli-Palestinian peace agreement.

And to my knowledge the Anti-Christ had been positively identified at least six times in my lifetime by 1993!

I knew as soon as any major earth event occurred that the usual suspects would begin their "End Times" catcalls.

And I was over it.

Cynicism had taken over.

My internal dialogue was running rampant.

Don't you guys see that natural disasters, wars, famine, pestilence, and all that business has been going down for centuries?

Don't you know that your "End Times" horn-blowing is eerily similar to the boy who cried wolf?

Don't you have anything better to do TODAY than get people all worked up over something for which no one knows the time?

It seemed as if I was against any semblance of an "End Times" ideology because of the people who comprised it, rather than seeking out a healthy kingdom approach shaped by Jesus' actual words.

I suppose that is more of a confession than anything.

But I think this illustrates one of the great divides we have within Christianity between the curious, the zealous, and the cynical.

And it is truly a divide.

The large majority of us are not really sure what to do with the "End Times."

Even worse, we have very little idea what Jesus had to say about the "End Times."

Even worse than that, we have absolutely no idea what Jesus wants us to do about the "End Times."

Interestingly enough, as I have traveled down this road, I have found that there are tons of people who have a mass of opinions about all of it though.

And all of these people have been influenced by multitudes of other people, who have a lot of different opinions themselves.

Sure, I suppose I could go down the path of evaluating every nuance of pre-tribulation rapture versus post-tribulation rapture.

Or, we could debate the merits of amillenialism versus preterism.

But to be honest, I am not that smart.

Nor do I have the energy for it.

And my guess is that there are many more people like me in this regard.

I would rather read *What Jesus Had to Say About the End Times for Dummies.*

Any takers?

Jesus was a man for simple people. He didn't make his messages incredibly complex. If you were a person that had the eyes to see and the ears to hear… then his message was easily understood.

And that is all I really care about.

What Jesus had to say about it and what Jesus wants us to do about it.

Plain and simple.

So, if Jesus really did have something to say about the "End Times"

And really did say something about how we ought to view such things

And how we ought to approach such things

And what our behaviors, actions, and priorities ought to be

Then maybe that is all we really need to know… without making it any more complex than that.

And I don't think it is too strong to say that *the message of Jesus is what we all should really want to know anyway.*

Nothing more, nothing less.

So while it is true that we could try to match up the books of Daniel and Revelation and try to figure out something new about "the beast"…

Or we could study the ancient language to try to figure out the exact "End Times" roadmap and the whole "End Times" checklist of what has already happened and what is supposed to happen next (and many do)… so what?

It's not like you are going to jump up and down and tell everyone around you that you got the play-by-play exactly right and that your theory was closest to being right when it all starts to go down.

C'mon.

The truth of the matter is that all of this will happen when it happens and the theories are inconsequential and who gets it right is of no concern.

The greater issue, that is way more important for all of us today, is: *Who are we becoming right now and who will we be if and when things become increasing chaotic and out of control?*

The greater issue, that is way more important for all of us today is not: *how we will escape the conflict of this world,* but rather: *how God will work through each of us in the middle of the conflict for His glory and His Kingdom purposes.*

That is what truly matters.

And that is what we will find matters to Jesus as well.

So whether you consider yourself curious, zealous, or wildly cynical and indifferent about the "End Times"...

Or, whether you consider yourself an average Joe who has never really considered anything at all to do with the "End Times," then this is for you.

What exactly did Jesus have to say about the "End Times" anyway?

_____

NUMBER ONE!

WARS, FAMINES, EARTHQUAKES, OH MY!

And you will hear of wars and rumors of wars; see that you are not frightened or troubled, for this must take place, but the end is not yet. For nation will rise against nation, and kingdom against kingdom, and there will be famines and earthquakes in place after place. All this is but the beginning [the early pains] of the birth pangs [of the intolerable anguish]. Then they will hand you over to suffer affliction and tribulation and put you to death, and you will be hated by all nations for My name's sake. Matthew 24: 6-9

I remember sitting in church service when I was 10-years old and my dad handing a King James pew bible to me.

It was opened to Matthew 24.

I took it from him as he whispered, "Read this."

"I can't. It's a King James Version," I quickly and wryly replied.

19

Ok. I didn't really say that.

But I bet I thought it!

Anyway... I took the old King James from his hand and settled into a comfortable reading position.

The red-lettered words of Jesus jumped off the page, as he responded to the *when* and *what* questions of the disciples, and it demanded my full attention.

Between the "thees" and "thous" and the "shalls" and "shall nots," I read what seemed to be describing the 1980's world in which I was living at the time.

Wars and rumors of war.
Nation fighting against nation.
Rulers fighting against rulers.
Famines.
Earthquakes.
Lions.
Tigers.
Bears.
Oh my!

It was heavy, heavy stuff.

And there was no question that it all seemed to me like birth pains of something bigger that could be coming at any moment.

Needless to say, that particular day made a huge impression on me.

How many ten-year-olds remember a specific Bible passage that they read on a specific day?

Not many.

There was something about that passage that made those ancient texts come to life. To me, they could have just as easily been written the day before.

They felt real and incredibly current.

And my guess is that had anyone asked me what specifically I remembered about what Jesus said to the disciples in Matthew 24, while sitting down for lunch at my Grandma's house after church, I would have said...

Wars.
Famines.
Earthquakes.

That would have been a no-brainer.

_____

Wars, famines, and earthquakes were things to which I could relate.

Not because I had been in the midst of any of it, but because that is what the news was littered with day after day.

Those were the things that kept me on the edge of my seat.
Those were the things that caused uncertainty and worry.
Those were the things that made this little 10-year-old a bit nervous.

So between reading Matthew 24, watching the news, and hearing others talk about the state of the world... the one thing that kept running through my mind was...

Could I be living in the "End Times?"

I even remember waking up in the middle of the night one time and looking out my bedroom window and up into the sky at the full moon.

It kinda had a reddish tinge to it.

Was it getting ready to turn to blood?

It's that kind of stuff that gets our minds running wild, which inevitably leads to a ton of uncertainty.

And a ton of uncertainty can lead to a litany of questions.

What would I do?
How would I respond?
Will I be ready?
Can I prepare?
Will I be wearing clean underwear?

————

But let's be honest.

Whether you consider yourself curious, zealous, cynical, or one who just doesn't care anything about the "End Times," you have to at least admit (at a minimum) that our circumstances can really make us act in ways we normally would not act.

That's not "End Times" talk.

That's just real life.

That's stuff we deal with every day.

For example.

I try to be a pretty good guy.

But when the dog pees on our kitchen floor (and he does).

22

I completely lose it.

A circumstance that I could not control (dog peeing on my kitchen floor) took place, and I behaved in a way that I would normally not behave (I completely lost my mind).

Forget Christ-likeness.

All semblance of sanity goes out the window, as my eyes roll back in my head and I start foaming gosh-darns at the mouth.

Love.
Joy.
Peace.
Patience.
Kindness.
Gentleness.
Self-Control.
All gone.

Christ-likeness? Buh-bye.

By virtue of something outside of my control, I allowed myself to devolve into a raging lunatic.

I didn't look much like Jesus.

And I know it isn't just me.

My buddy Patrick wants to be like Jesus, but he gets really angry when people ride his bumper while driving.

My buddy Josh wants to be like Jesus, but he gets frustrated with people at work and handles his frustration in ways he later regrets.

My buddy Herb wants to be like Jesus, but sometimes he is really judgmental and not very loving toward people who say or do really stupid things.

My boys and I aren't weird or abnormal.

Well, Herb is a little weird.

But that is another story.

So it may be more accurate to say that for the most part, we aren't too weird.

But anyway.

I think we are representative of most people who follow Jesus.

We want to be like Jesus but at times we allow our circumstances to dictate our behavior.

_____

We let outside variables affect us and then we behave in ways that are far from the richness and fullness of Christ.

We let outside variables affect us in ways that completely rob us of love, joy, peace, and contentment.

And believe me... it completely stinks.

But I don't want you to miss the point here.

There's no denying that we all really do want to be like Jesus, through and through.

We all really do want the Spirit of God to be an active part of restoring and making us completely new from the inside out.

And, we all really do want to consistently put that life on display through thick and thin for the world to see.

We are completely committed to following Jesus in every single part of our lives.

But sometimes we let situations and circumstances get the best of us.

And we revert back to attitudes, actions, and behaviors that fall short of who Christ is making us to be.

But we don't just throw our arms up in the air in defeat and live as if we will always let circumstances compromise our pursuit to live like Jesus.

We meet together every single week and we confess our sins to one another.

We recognize and readily admit the areas of our lives in which we have displayed anything less than Christ.

And we move forward in confidence that those old ways are being put to death and the Spirit of God is breathing a new way of life inside each of us.

No matter our situation or circumstance.

Together.

We resolve to be like Jesus.

———

So what on earth does any of this have to do with the "End Times?"

Surprisingly, way more than you might think.

While it's true that we can't control the situations that happen around us... *we can absolutely control our own attitudes, actions, and behaviors.*

And I honestly don't know of any truth that is more important than that.

Presently, or as times grow more complex and more uncertain, we have a choice in our attitudes, actions, and behavior.

In economic collapse.
or civil unrest.
or lawlessness.
or wars.
or earthquakes.
or famines.
or persecution.
or the moon turning to blood!

Our circumstances ought not dictate us.
Our circumstances ought not control us.
Our circumstances ought not influence us.

We have a choice in who we are going to be.

And we have a choice in how we respond to the circumstances that surround us.

Even, and especially, when life begins to look like it is coming apart at the seams.

Even when all we hear are the possibilities of everything collapsing around us.

Even when the ground of stability begins to shake beneath our feet.

We have a choice.

Who are we going to be?

That is the most important and most essential question that has to be asked.

Because the people we will be tomorrow begins with the path we are walking today.

And the people we will be tomorrow begins with the people with whom we choose to walk alongside today.

And the people we will be tomorrow is determined by how we help each other travel this narrow path today.

And by today I mean... *today.*

Like right now.

_____

If I had a trumpet that you could hear right now,

I would blow it.

The chapter two processional has reached the destination we have been moving toward.

So imagine horns.

Triumphant horns at that.

All the wars, earthquakes, and famine business?

Yeah.

Jesus had something to say about all that.

(Horns blowing triumphantly)

27

Here it is! Wait for it. Wait for it.

Jesus said not to be worried, or alarmed, or frightened, or troubled by any of it.

That's right.

He said not to be worried, or alarmed, or frightened, or troubled.
In fact...

He said that all these things have to happen.
He said that we should absolutely expect them to happen.
He said they are just the beginning of something that is yet to come.

He called them the *birth pains of the Messiah.*

They are sharp and intense and increasing in frequency.

And in the same way that birth pains precede the arrival of a baby,

So the birth pains of creation must precede the arrival of the Christ.

But don't worry, be happy.

In fact, be joyous!

And in the meantime (and then in the meantime after that),

Just chill.

And be joyous some more!

Easier said than done, I know.

But you wanted to know what Jesus had to say, right?

I have faithfully walked alongside my wife through three pregnancies.

Through the nausea.
Through the headaches.
Through the swollen feet.
Through the nighttime restlessness.
Through all of the physical discomfort.

And through the increasingly powerful contractions leading up to the births of our children.

And despite all of the pain and discomfort, longing and tears, there was profound anticipation and excitement and joy through it all.

I remember vividly the days of their arrival.
I remember seeing them for the first time.
I remember tears welling up in my eyes in humility, amazement, joy, and love.

Whatever we had been through up to now... was worth this moment (at least that is what my wife said... and I trust her... because she is the one who did all of the work).

But that is the truth.

It was worth it more than words could ever describe.

And that is precisely why Jesus used the metaphor of pregnancy, because it masterfully described what the conditions would be like before the End of the Age and before his arrival.

Yes, of course there will be pain.
Yes, of course there will be discomfort.
Yes, of course there will be restlessness.

And it may feel like agony.
And it may make you want to scream.

But do not fear. Do not stress. Do not give up. Do not lose heart.

Because the hardship and pain will be so
sweet and rich and beautiful and poetic
in light of the birth of new creation
and the presence of the Messiah.

And the tears that will be shed will be tears of humility, amazement,
joy, and love.

Not tears of sorrow.

For the tears of sorrow will have been wiped away.

So be patient. Be content. Be joyful.

All in hope.

Amen.

_____

But can we be honest here?

Just a little bit?

Just between you and me?

When it comes to all of this "End Times" talk, all of this "End Times"
study, and all of this "End Times" mania that goes on…

All I keep hearing is everyone's opinion about how it is going to go
down and what we need to do to prepare for it.

And to be really honest... I haven't heard anyone talk about the important stuff.

I haven't heard one person talk about the importance of being people who don't wig out, not just presently, but when the doo doo hits the fan.

I haven't heard one person talk about the importance of being people who are not worried and who are not alarmed, frightened, or troubled, not just presently, but when it gets really crazy and chaotic.

I haven't heard one person talk about the absolute necessity of us being Jesus to the world, not just presently, but even and especially when times grow more uncertain and people are looking desperately for an ounce of hope.

I only hear people talking about what signs to look for and what canned goods we ought to stock and why we need freeze dried meals and how much gold we ought to have on hand and which guns we need to buy to protect ourselves and how much ammo we ought to have and what kind of power generator is the best and I just wonder, I just wonder, I just wonder...

Is it that easy to throw away everything Jesus taught us?

Is it that easy to turn away from everything he has made us to be?

Is it that easy to begin trusting ourselves rather than God?

And is it that easy to sacrifice who he wants us to be in and for an out-of-control world?

Is it really that easy?

_____

Yes, I understand that our natural inclination, our human tendency, is to *freak out* when we feel like we are losing control.

Yes, the circumstances around us can very easily influence or affect our attitudes, actions, and behaviors.

Yes, uncertainty can pull us toward anxiety, worry, and fear.

And yes, as times grow more uncertain, we can very easily begin putting our hope, our faith, and our trust in ourselves.

I get it.

It's easy.

The less control we believe we have in a situation, the more out-of-control we feel.

When the walls feel like they are closing in around us, we don't feel like there is anything we can do about it.

So we take matters into our own hands.

And we tend to gravitate toward things that we *can* control.

We do those things that we believe will reduce our stress, anxiety, and fear levels.

And we pursue those things that offer security.

But the truth is… *we completely sell out in the process*.

The truth is that we begin to completely abandon our faith in God.

The truth is that we no longer trust in God and God alone.

The truth is that we believe that we are better than God to handle the unknown.

The truth is that we believe we have a better idea of how to reduce our stress, anxiety, and fear than God does.

The truth is that we believe our own security is more important than the identity and purpose God has for us in the world.

And we compromise.
And compromise.
And compromise.

Identity lost.
Purpose lost.

Rather than being the embodiment of faith and hope in the midst of uncertainty...

(WHICH IS NEEDED AND WILL CONTINUE TO BE DESPERATELY NEEDED)

We instead operate from a place of fear, anxiety, worry, and insecurity.

Like everyone else.

And we become something far less than what Christ has been making us to be and has always intended us to be.

Through the thick.
Through the thin.

We trust ourselves.

Not God.

———

But the echoes of Jesus' words cannot be suppressed or erased or minimized.

They haunt.
They pursue.

They pierce.

And they cannot be shaken.

As much as we may try to run or hide or escape the truth… his words will be right there with us.

And we will still hear him saying…

Do not worry or be anxious about tomorrow, for tomorrow will have it's own worries and anxieties.[1]

Do not be anxious and troubled with cares about your life, as to what you will eat, or about your body, as to what you will wear.[2]

Do not become alarmed and panic-stricken and terrified.[3]

Do not let your hearts be troubled, distressed, or agitated. You believe in and adhere to and trust in and rely on God; believe in and adhere to and trust in and rely also on me.[4]

Do not be seized with alarm and struck with fear, little flock, for it is your Father's good pleasure to give you the kingdom![5]

I am here and I will be with you.
Even until the End of the Age.[6]

―――――――

While it is true that the people we will be tomorrow begins with the path we are walking today,

And while it is true that the people we will be tomorrow begins with the people whom we choose to walk alongside today,

And while it is true that the people we will be tomorrow is determined by how we help each other travel this narrow path today,

We have to be honest with ourselves.

On exactly what path are we walking?

What kind of people have we chosen to walk alongside?

And how are we helping each other walk this narrow path of hope, faith, and trust in God, looking more like Jesus each day of our lives, as things become progressively more uncertain?

These questions are so vitally important.

But the answers are even more important.

Can you say that no matter your situation or circumstance that you and the people you are walking alongside resolve to be like Jesus?

Can you say that no matter your situation or circumstance you and the people you are walking alongside resolve to trust him in everything?

Can you say that no matter your situation or circumstance you and the people you are walking alongside trust him with your lives?

Can you say that no matter your situation or circumstance you and the people you are walking alongside trust him through thick or thin?

Can you say that no matter your situation or circumstance you and the people you are walking alongside trust him through the highs and the lows?

Can you say that no matter your situation or circumstance you and the people you are walking alongside trust him in life or in death?

Sure these are tough questions.

But if we are those who really, truly follow the way of Jesus, we take his every word and every action to heart.

His way is our way.

Even if it means our lives.

Period.

‾‾‾‾

NUMBER TWO!

THE COSMIC GENIE

Then the kingdom of God shall be likened to ten virgins who took their lamps and went to meet the bridegroom. Matthew 25: 1

The kingdom of God is like a man who was about to take a long journey and he called his servants together and entrusted them with his property. Matthew 25:14

All nations will be gathered before Him, and He will separate them [the people] from one another as a shepherd separates his sheep from the goats. Matthew 25: 32

Do you ever get the sense that we Christians, might have our orientation a bit wrong?

You know.

Like.

The sun circling the earth.
Rather than the earth circling the sun.

That kinda thing.

Sometimes I just wonder.

Do we believe that God revolves around us?
Or, do we believe that we revolve around God?

These are staggering questions.

Who is at the center?

Are we at the center?

Or, is God at the center?

The way we answer that question alters the entire universe.

In a universe where we operate as if we are at the center and where God revolves around us, God is placed in an inferior, subservient position to us.

It is a God-works-for-us mentality, in which God is more like our genie in a bottle, and we are more like the masters.

It is an orientation that believes God's intention and purpose is to work on our behalf.

Serve us.
Make us comfortable.
Give us more possessions.
Get us out of tough spots.
And keep us from getting hurt.

Think I have gone too far?

Just listen to our prayers.

———

Of course later in history we figured out that the earth, in fact, does revolve around the sun.

Thanks to that nasty ol' heretic Copernicus.

He got in some trouble for that discovery.

The Roman Catholic Church got completely ticked at him, because his discovery took earth and humankind… out of the center.

Ironic, huh?

And in the same way that his discovery led to a scientific revolution and a complete reshaping and reorienting of how we view our position and relationship to the sun, I truly believe that we are on the cusp of an even greater revolution.

And it begins by each one of us realizing our position and our relationship with God.

This alone has the potential to reshape and reorient our priorities and what we view as important, giving us a newfound identity and purpose.

And it is as simple as acknowledging and living our lives with God as the center.

Not ourselves.

The entire created order, including humanity, was created to revolve around God.

Not around us.

This change in thinking, this reorientation, when it happens, will have profound implications for our lives and for the world.

But it means that we have to discard any and all of the beliefs, convictions, and notions that came about as a result of our misguided idea that God revolved around us in the first place.

And our beginning point is prayer.

Rather than continuing with prayers that make our pursuits and our interests the center, let us make God and God's kingdom the center around which we live and move.

_____

Our Father who is in heaven
Hallowed be your name.

Your kingdom come,
Your will be done
on earth as it is in heaven.

Give us this day our daily bread.
And forgive us our debts,
as we also have forgiven
And lead us not into temptation,
but deliver us from the evil one.

For Yours is the kingdom
and the power
and the glory forever.

Amen.

_____

When God is at the center, we are completely preoccupied with...

God's interests.
God's plans.
God's intentions.
God's will.
God's way.
God's reign.
God's kingdom.

Period.

Our interests.
Our plans.
Our intentions.
Our will.
Our way.
Our reign.
Our own kingdom.

Are completely inconsequential.

Our lives.
Our pursuits.
Our orientations.
Our priorities.
Our values.
Our allegiances.
Our opinions.
Our preoccupations.
Our inclinations.
Our principles.
Our entire world.
And our very core existence…

Are all predicated and oriented around one thing, and one thing alone…

God.

Period.

This is not a cause for shock or sadness, but the opportunity for joy and celebration.

For this is the way it was always gloriously meant to be.

God at the center and all of creation encircling in praise.

———

So rather than treating God as a cosmic genie working only for our benefit, as we reorient, we begin to see God rightly as Redeemer, Reconciler, and Restorer of all things.

We move from God-in-a-box to God encompassing all things, including the box.

We move from a God with singular and narrow purpose to a God with expansive and all-encompassing purpose.

We move from a God whose only intention is to rescue us and take us to heaven, to a God who, instead, generously invites us into his richness and fullness and then entrusts us to extend that richness and fullness in his redemptive work of the world.

Rather than the centerpiece being us, and God revolving around us for our purposes, God is the centerpiece around which we revolve and live for his purposes.

With this reorientation, we no longer lose sight of the larger story itself.

And this is where we, once again, begin to circle the wagon.

This is where everything begins to come into full view.

When God is at the supreme center of everything...

We begin to navigate through the 150 pages in the middle.

We begin to enter the development of the plot.

We begin to face the conflict head-on with God leading the way.

We begin to seek out and embrace our character development.

We begin to find our rhythm, our movement, our purpose.

And we begin to discover the beauty and the drama of our own narrative.

This is a fascinating realization, because the competing Christian narrative does not sound anything like this.

In fact, it sounds more like the sun revolving around the earth.

It has been a narrative in which we are at the center and God is working for our interests and our purposes.

God, hurry up and rescue me because everything is getting really bad down here.

This world is so terrible; I wish it would just end.

Jesus, I am just waiting for you to call my name and take me away.

God, why did Hostess have to go out of business?

These are real statements that I have heard in the last few months from real people.

It is a position that screams more *My Kingdom Come, My Will Be Done* than anything else.

It is a position that begins with your interests, your well-being, and your wants, needs, and desires rather than that of God's.

_____

So reorientation is essential.

God-centered people do not start with what *they want* but with what *God wants.*

Through the good times and the bad.

We do not get to pick and choose.

It is not *what we want in the situation* or *how we can escape it...* but how God wants to use us.

God-centered people do not view the world as something to escape, but as something that God is redeeming.

Even, and especially, when the love of so many will grow increasingly cold.

God-centered people do not believe their purpose on earth is to "make a decision for Christ" and then wait for him to take them away, but rather *to be those who are at work presently to ready the world for his return.*

Come hell or high water.

And that is a HUGE DIFFERENCE between the two perspectives.

God-centered people are those who work on behalf of God as faithful servants presently.

Whether his return is tomorrow or a thousand years from now.

God-centered people are faithful, thoughtful, and wise in their work.

Whether they have been given much or little.

44

God-centered people are those who do well with what has been entrusted to them.

And this is not my opinion.

These are the words of Jesus.

When he spoke in parables about the virgins.

When he spoke in parables about the servants and the Master.

And when he spoke metaphorically about the sheep and the goats.

_____

Parables bring forth truths hidden since the creation of the world.

However, in the parables, these truths are not always apparent.

Only those who have the eyes to see that truth… can see it.

Only those who have the ears to hear that truth… can hear it.

But many times people read or hear the parables and completely miss the point.

This was the case, after one particular parable, in which Jesus did not explain it to the people.

And as he left the crowds his disciples asked him why he did not explain it.

He said.

Because the knowledge of the secrets of the kingdom of God has been given to you… but not to them.

45

And so it began.

In parables.

Truths hidden since the creation of the world.

About the knowledge of the secrets of the kingdom of God.

Sown.
Planted.
Conferred.
Given.
Entrusted.

To those who were closest to Jesus.
To those who had the eyes to see.
To those who had the ears to hear.
To those who would be faithful with it.
To those who would be thoughtful with it.
To those who would be wise in what they do with it.
To those who could be trusted with it.
To those who would give everything they have to attain it.
To those who would further sow it.
To those who would take it to others as a blessing.

———

Here is a parable.

About ten virgins.[7]

Who are going out to meet the bridegroom in order to accompany him and the wedding processional to the Marriage Feast.

Five foolish virgins take only their lamps.

Five wise virgins take their lamps and extra oil.

But the bridegroom for whom they were waiting was delayed.

And the night fell.

And it grew darker as they continued to wait.

And their lamps continued to burn in the darkness.

At midnight, there was a shout, *Go out to meet the bridegroom!*

But because the lamps burned into the night, the five foolish virgins did not have enough oil to meet the bridegroom.

So they left in order to purchase more oil.

However, the wise virgins had plenty of oil.

They had worked ahead and planned wisely.

They refilled their lamps and then left to meet and accompany the bridegroom, the bride, and the wedding processional.

When they arrived at the marriage feast... the doors were closed behind them and the celebration began.

So when the foolish virgins arrived knocking at the door... the bridegroom replied, *I am not acquainted with you.*

The knowledge of the secrets of the kingdom of God is revealed in this parable and is instructive for us today.

In the kingdom of God,

The sensible.
The wise.
The prudent.

Eagerly anticipate the arrival of the bridegroom

and make wise provision to keep their light of good works shining for they know not when the Bridegroom might arrive.

Even in the darkest hour,

The sensible.
The wise.
The prudent.

Keep their light shining.
So when they hear the shout of his arrival,
they may greet him and join the wedding processional
into the great banquet hall of the Marriage Feast celebration.

This is the truth of God hidden since the creation of the world.

_____

Another parable.

A master was leaving for a long journey.
He called together his servants.

And entrusted them with money, each according to his ability.[8]

The servant who was given five talents traded and earned an additional five talents.

The servant who was given two talents traded and earned an additional two talents.

The servant who was given one talent... buried it.

After a long period of time, the master returned.

To the first servant he commended him for being honorable and trustworthy.

To the second servant he commended him as he did the first.

To the third servant he condemned him for being lazy and idle with what he was given.

The knowledge of the secrets of the kingdom of God is revealed in this parable and is instructive for us today.

In the kingdom of God,

The honorable.
The trustworthy.
The admirable.

Make wise investments on that which is given and entrusted to them by the Master.

And, each is given according to his individual ability.

The knowledge of the secrets of the kingdom of God has been entrusted to the servants of God in order to grow and extend God's reign on earth presently before the return of the Master.

This is the truth of God hidden since the creation of the world.

_____

The words of Christ are clear.

No one will know the day or time of his return.

No one.

No how.

No way.

He will come like a thief in the night.

And thieves do not call before they break into your house.

They come when you least expect it.

At least that is what my friends who are thieves say.
Wink. Wink.

But for those who consider themselves

The pure.
The clean.
The holy.

The entrusted servants of God.

Many things are clear from the parables of Jesus.

Responsibility has been given to us presently, while he is not with us, to be sensible, wise, and prudent… until he returns.

Responsibility has been given to us presently, while he is not with us, to keep the light of our good works shining even through the darkest hours… until he returns.

Responsibility has been given to us presently, while he is not with us, to take what has been entrusted to each of us and put it to good use so as to extend God's reign on earth… until he returns.

The parables of Jesus are clear and unambiguous that we are to be at work presently on his behalf until he returns.

This is precisely what God's kingdom and God's reign looks like on earth.

But to avoid confusion.
To avoid abstraction.
To avoid excuses.

Jesus follows up his parables by saying,

Here is how I am going to break this thing down.
Here is how I am going to make my judgment.
Here is how I will decide who my true servants were while I was
gone.

You are either a sheep or a goat.[9]

How does that hit you?

A sheep.

A goat.

Right hand.

Left hand.

Favored.

Not favored.

Kingdom.

No Kingdom.

And the differences between the two?

The sheep are those servants of Christ who are sensible, wise,
prudent, honorable, trustworthy, and admirable, in that while Christ
was away and even in the darkest hour, they let their light of good
works shine in the darkness by feeding the hungry, giving drink to
the thirsty, welcoming and giving shelter to the homeless, clothing
the naked, and visiting and caring for the sick and imprisoned.

The goats are those who are thoughtless, lazy, and idle. And though
they claim to be a servant of Christ while he is away, they do not

take prudent steps to ensure that their light of good works continue to shine in the darkest hour before the Master's return. The goats are those who have been entrusted a portion of the kingdom of God and bury it for fear of the Master, neglecting the cause of the hungry, the thirsty, the homeless, the naked, and the sick and imprisoned.

The parables of Jesus show us what our lives look like when God is at the center.

———

Those who are worried that this looks like an attempt at "earning one's salvation" should not fret.

It is because of the graceful generosity of the One who entrusted us with his kingdom that we are compelled and overjoyed to work on his behalf.

It is because of the One who delivers and saves that those in darkness will see a great light, as we carry the light of Christ into the darkness and await the coming of Christ the Bridegroom.

It is because of the One who has taken us from great bondage and into great freedom that we wholeheartedly proclaim the freedom message of the King and his kingdom to the world.

Our salvation compels us to extend it to the world.

And it is our honor.

I believe this is where a great synergy begins to takes place.

From the *when* and *what* questions of the "End Times" to the reframed and reoriented question of, "Who are you making us to be?"

From the worry, stress, and anxiety of uncertain times, to the peaceful contentment and joy of knowing that Christ is with us in both easy and difficult times.

From a place of idle waiting and missing opportunities, while the bags are packed so "Jesus can come to take us away," to a place of embracing this blessed and full life and extending it to everyone in our midst.

From cynicism and indifference when hearing anything related to the "End Times", to hopeful anticipation of our Savior's return and the renewal of all things.

This is the place where we all come together as one – the curious, the zealous, the cynical, and the indifferent.

Where our own individual narratives become one single narrative.

Where our voices singing in isolation come together in unison as a resounding heavenly chorus.

Where the individual instruments we play join together in the fullness of a wonderfully orchestrated symphony.

And it is with a renewed sense that we are to have a singular identity in the world together.

And it is with a renewed sense that we are to have a unified purpose together in the present, even as things become increasingly complex and chaotic.

But we are only scratching the surface.

For we will need to know who we are and to what purpose we are being called as we stand together before the great global challenge in front of us.

NUMBER THREE!

FREE FILL DIRT

And this gospel of the kingdom will be preached in the whole world as a testimony to all nations, and then the end will come. Matthew 24: 14

I have been especially coy with the title of this book.

AND THEN THE END WILL COME!

Yes, it's completely over the top.

ALL CAPS.

And an exclamation mark!

I have to admit… it's a bit out of character for me.

I am way more lower case and periods.

But as I mentioned at the beginning, the title captures all the hype and hysteria we give to anything "End Times."

And I was poking some fun at it.

Not a lot of poking.

Just a little poking.

And not mean poking.

Fun poking.

Know what I mean?

But there is even more to it than all of that.

If there is a funny side with the ALL CAPS and the exclamation mark and all of the over-the-topness that it exudes… then there is also a much more poignant side.

But let's not be too methodical here.

Let's just be anecdotal.

Over the last few weeks I have mentioned or shown the title of this book to over two baker's dozens worth of people (that would be over 26 people)… and after their complete shock that a guy like me would be writing an "End Times" book… I asked them if the title rings a bell.

By asking such a broad question I was never really surprised when no one had any idea that the title had any real significance other than being completely over the top.

But then I got more specific.

I asked them if they remembered ever seeing that phrase in the context of Jesus talking about wars, rumors of wars, earthquakes, and famines.

Ah yes! Of course!

With a hint like that... every single person suddenly began to remember.

Oh! Yeah yeah. Earthquakes. Yeah yeah yeah... I remember all that!

And you thought I was kidding in Chapter 2.

People always remember the earthquakes and the other crazy stuff.

But they hardly remember the really important stuff that surrounds all the crazy stuff.

In fact, I was about to make that exact point with my friends.

_____

But before we get to that.

The entire concept of this book is rooted in this one single point that I was about to make with my friends.

And, it was this one single point that changed my entire "End Times" perspective.

But not just that.

It was this one single point that changed the entire trajectory of my faith.

57

It was this one single point that changed my entire perspective as to why I am alive.

It was this one single point that changed my identity and my purpose in this life.

It was this one single point that completely changed me from the inside-out.

I could hardly believe it.
I could hardly conceive of the implications.
I could hardly imagine what this would mean, not just for me, but also more broadly for followers of Jesus.

_____

What I found, from all of my discussions with my friends, is that we, as Christians, have a much better grasp (and get way more excited) about what follows the "AND" than about what precedes the "AND."

AND THEN THE END WILL COME!

But what exactly precedes that?

We love all the talk and chatter and speculation about the end coming.

But what is it that comes before the "AND" anyway?

And why don't we know it like the back of our hand?

And why isn't it that part that we are completely obsessed with?

And why isn't it that part that we get really, really excited about?

And why isn't it that part that dominates sermon topics and books and movies?

And why isn't it that part that shapes how we see everything else that Jesus said about the "End Times?"

You would think that *anything at all* that precedes the words *AND THEN THE END WILL COME* would automatically be the absolute focus and obsession of everyone who follows Jesus.

You might also think that anything at all that precedes the words *AND THEN THE END WILL COME* could potentially be some of the most important words of Jesus in all the Gospels.

Ever.

Words he might want us to know.
Words he might want us to take to heart.
Words he might want us to do something about.

Because it precedes the "End" coming.

So without further delay.

This is what I told my friends.

Jesus, when speaking to the disciples about wars and earthquakes and famines and chaos and lawlessness and birth pains and afflictions and death, said:

And the Good News (the Gospel) of the kingdom will be preached throughout the whole world as a testimony to all the nations, AND THEN THE END WILL COME!

———

It was at this place in the conversation where everyone said in a surprised tone, "Oh!"

And then I asked, "So what exactly IS the Good News of the kingdom?"

Only to hear everyone say in a solemn tone, "Oh."

Yeah. Oh.

Like Uh-oh.

_____

Some may say that the Church has already been preaching the Good News (the Gospel) of the death, burial, and resurrection of Jesus Christ all around the world for a long time.

So what's the big deal?

Well, I have one all-important question.

And it is essential that you follow me here.

Being that the Bible documents Jesus preaching the Good News (the Gospel) BEFORE his death, burial, and resurrection...

How can the Gospel that the Church has been preaching ONLY focus on the death, burial, and resurrection?

Did you get that?

Jesus was preaching the Good News (Gospel) before his death, yet the only Good News (Gospel) that we preach is his death, burial, and resurrection.

The Good News (Gospel) that Jesus preached *could not have included his death, burial, and resurrection.*

(Because he was still alive)

Have you ever thought about that?

Jesus was preaching the Good News (the Gospel) BEFORE he even died.[10]

Jesus was preaching the Good News (the Gospel) BEFORE his burial.

Jesus was preaching the Good News (the Gospel) BEFORE his resurrection.

Which means the ONLY conclusion we can reach is that the Good News (the Gospel) has to be more than only the death, burial, and resurrection of Jesus Christ.

Yes!

The Good News is MORE than just the death, burial, and resurrection of Jesus!

What a profound realization and an earth-shattering revelation.

While so many within the Church have been preaching only the Good News of the death, burial, and resurrection ... there is surprisingly so much more!

And, while so much time and attention has been given to theories and speculation about the "End Times" and the future and how it is all going to go down... there is a present reality... a present task... that demands our full attention.

A present reality that is more important than anything related to the "End Times."

In fact, a present reality that is more important than anything else that we might preoccupy ourselves.

And it is, as Jesus said, *the Good News of the kingdom*.

Read the words of Jesus again.

*And the **Good News (the Gospel) of the kingdom** will be preached throughout the whole world as a testimony to all the nations, AND THEN THE END WILL COME!*

The Good News (the Gospel) that Jesus preached was the...

Good News of the kingdom!

Not just the Good News of his death, burial, and resurrection.

The Good News of... AGAIN... the kingdom.

And it WILL BE PREACHED to all the nations.

And if we do not have any idea what the kingdom is... then how will we ever preach it to the world?

This is really heavy, heavy stuff.

But also cause for great celebration and excitement.

Is it possible that we could potentially be on the cusp of discovering something that is ridiculously revolutionary, desperately needed, and that will absolutely rock the foundations of the world?

I say yes.

And believe me, I can say it even more emphatically than that!

YES!

_____

So what exactly did Jesus have to say about this ridiculously revolutionary, desperately needed, world-altering message of the kingdom?

What did he have to say about this message that will be preached to all the nations before the "End" comes?

Well.

Jesus said that the very reason he came to earth in the first place... *was to preach the message of the kingdom.*

Did you catch that?

The REASON he came.

In fact, this kingdom message is so important that it was what Jesus talked about more than anything else throughout his ministry.

More than anything else!

This kingdom message was so important that he even preached it for the forty days after his resurrection.[11]

Yes.

For all forty days after his resurrection before he ascended to heaven... he preached the kingdom.

That should at least begin to underscore the importance of this kingdom message.

It was the reason he came.
It was his primary message before he died.
And it was his most important message even after his resurrection.

But there is so much more.

Jesus described the kingdom throughout his entire ministry in parables.

That's right.

Parables.

Truths hidden since the creation of the world.

Truths not readily apparent to just anyone.

Truths that require "the eyes to see and ears to hear" to understand them.

Which again means that many people will not understand (or have not understood) the kingdom message... and will miss it.

For as we have not understood the parables,
We have missed the truths hidden since the creation of the world,
which are the truths of the kingdom.

And that's why so many have missed the kingdom.

Because we have not been looking for it.

———

Please don't get lost in all the details.

It is really this simple.

Despite the primary message of Jesus being the kingdom... we have missed it.

But it is the kingdom that will be preached to all the nations AND THEN THE END WILL COME!

And right now as we speak, there is a gap between the two.

We don't know how to talk about the kingdom.

Because we simply don't know it.

_____

I listened to a guy preach recently.

He preached to over a thousand people at an established church.

His sermon was about the Good News (the Gospel).

And he was wildly passionate about it.

He preached for a full hour.

Pacing back and forth.

Probably even sweating.

And never once mentioned the kingdom.

NEVER.

ONCE.

MENTIONED.

THE.

KINGDOM.

WHEN.

PREACHING.

THE.

GOOD.

NEWS.

FOR.

AN.

HOUR.

Not once.

This is true.

He preached a message about the Good News and NEVER once mentioned the kingdom!

He only kept referring to the Good News as the death, burial, and resurrection of Jesus.

Which I agree with... partly.

But as I shared with you earlier...

We know that Jesus preached the Gospel BEFORE he even died... so where is the rest of the Good News (the Gospel)?

Where is this message of the kingdom that Jesus preached?

It's missing.

———

Here is a good way to think about it.

Because the death, burial, and resurrection are vitally important to the Good News, let's say that the death, burial, and resurrection of Jesus is the exclamation mark.

But not the whole sentence.

The kingdom message is the entire sentence.

And if we are ever going to understand the kingdom and then preach it to the world… we are going to have to understand *the entire sentence… not just the exclamation mark!*

_____

So let's talk about the entire sentence… the kingdom message.

Jesus described the kingdom in many different ways through many different parables.

He said that the kingdom is like seeds falling on the ground… but only taking root and growing in the fertile soil of one's life.[12]

He said the kingdom is like a treasure hidden in a field… that a person would sell everything to attain it.[13]

He said the kingdom is like a valuable pearl set among lesser jewels… that a person would sell everything to purchase it.[14]

In other words, the kingdom is incomparably rich and incredibly valuable, but one must seek it out and have his or her heart and mind open to receive it.

He said the kingdom is like the smallest of all seeds (the mustard seed)… but it grows and invasively takes over everything in its path.[15]

He said the kingdom is like yeast in dough… and as the dough is worked the yeast spreads throughout the entire batch.[16]

He said the kingdom is like a man who sowed good seed but while he was sleeping his enemy came and sowed weeds… and the wheat grew up among the weeds.[17]

He said the kingdom is like a net that is lowered into the lake… and when the net is pulled up it catches both good and bad fish to be sorted out later.[18]

The kingdom is small, but once it takes root and begins to work it's way out in our lives... it completely takes over and grows and spreads among the weeds of the world. In the end, it is God who sorts out the wheat and the weeds and the good and the bad fish.

And while those parables are incredibly insightful descriptions of how the kingdom breaks into the present-day reality of our lives and spreads throughout the weeds of the world...

It doesn't say much about what the kingdom actually is.

So if the kingdom really is something the entire world will need to hear before the return of Christ.

And if the kingdom really is like a light in the darkness.

Then it must be something that is completely contrary to the way of the world.

It must be something that is radically different than the current way we live and operate.

And it must be something that is completely life altering and world shaking.

This kingdom message must be something that is full of so much love and so much life that there is no conceivable way anyone could possibly resist it.

That is why it is essential that we know and live it and preach it.

_____

So let's take another step.

Jesus said that *this kingdom* is *within you.*[19]

And by that he meant that it could never be seen.

Nor could it ever be destroyed.

It is a present, inward reality in your life.

And already, that is the kind of thing of which I would like to take part.

Because every kingdom I have ever heard of could be taken over.

Every single kingdom I have ever heard of could be destroyed.

However... a kingdom inside of me that can never be taken over or destroyed is...

INCREDIBLE.

Sign me up.

But Jesus even went further.

He said that this kingdom and it's values...

Don't look anything like the values we see in this world.

In fact, they don't look like anything the world has ever seen before.

Because they happen to be the very values of God.

Yes.

The very values of God.

In us.

This kingdom.
This treasure.

This valuable pearl.

That we have discovered.
That we have given up everything to attain.

This inward reality.
This seed planted in our lives.
This seed that begins to grow and take over.

That will never be seen.
That will never be destroyed.
That operates by a different value system.
The very value system of God.

Is God's presence.
God's reign.
God's rule.
God's Spirit.

IN OUR LIVES!

———

Jesus said that the values of this counter-cultural kingdom look like this:

When you get hit, turn your cheek.
When someone is burdening you, go an extra mile.
When someone takes everything you have, give them even more.
When someone is angry with you, forgive and keep forgiving them.

When people are tearing you apart, don't get angry but love them.
When people are only out for themselves, be selfless and look out for others.
When people are judgmental, stand beside those who are being judged.
When people push others away as outcasts or sinners, befriend the outcast.

When someone powers over you, remain a humble servant.
When someone wants to be seen and glorified, take an unseen position.
When someone puts on a good show but is corrupt, be pure from the inside-out.
When someone is unjust and unmerciful, be just and merciful no matter what.

When people fight wars, stand on the side of peace all the time.
When people insult, ridicule, and curse you, bless them instead.
When people assault you, do not resist them for the sake of peace.
When people beat you and spit upon you and want to crucify you, lovingly forgive them and be willing to go to your death demonstrating the love of God.

It is this kind of character.
It is this kind of disposition.
It is this kind of behavior.

That is the embodiment of God's value system, God's reign, God's kingdom.

It is a life that is willing to go all the way to death to prove just how much you love.

To those who are worthy and to those who are unworthy.

And it always, always, always, always, always, always, always looks like Jesus.

That is the kingdom.

That through God's loving, forgiving, merciful grace... a completely different life is possible.

Not just in Jesus.

But for us as well.

A life of freedom.
A life of liberation.
A life of richness.
A life of fullness.

Not by the world's definition.

But by God's.

And it's available.

Right now.

Today.

As we breathe.

And with every single breath.

A full life is possible.

A life of richness is possible.

A life of freedom is possible.

_____

And this kingdom always seems like the most unconventional path.

It never seems to make sense in an increasingly upside-down world.

It looks like being poor in spirit.
It looks like humility.
It looks like meekness.

It looks like long-suffering.
It looks like mourning at the tension in the world.
It looks like longing for righteousness.
It looks like giving mercy.
It looks like being pure in heart.
It looks like being peaceful.
It looks like being persecuted for doing all these things.

And it looks like Jesus in everything we do.

Love.
Joy.
Peace.
Patience.
Kindness.
Gentleness.
Self-Control.

When times are easy.

And when times are so difficult that it seems like you will break.

It is breaking and pouring ourselves out for the...

Hungry.
Thirsty.
Homeless.
Naked.
Sick.
Imprisoned.
Marginalized.
Down-trodden.
Over-burdened.
And hopeless people in the world.

Friend and enemy alike.

And that, my friends, is the sentence!

With the punctuation that validates and brings life to the entire sentence being the exclamation mark of Christ's death, burial, and resurrection.

For without his death, burial, and resurrection...

The sentence would be inconsequential.

But the exclamation mark by itself without the sentence would be incomplete as well.

Look how glorious and rich a treasure is found in the magnificence of the sentence and the exclamation.

_____

I used to travel a twenty-mile stretch of road for my job.

And I traveled it once a week.

On this route there was a strange coincidence I didn't initially notice.

In fact.

It took me several months to pay enough attention to make the connection.

At some point in traveling this road I noticed a sign that read...

NEED FILL DIRT

Being one who lived about 60 miles from that location... I didn't find it incredibly relevant to my life situation.

Nor did I have any fill dirt to spare.

But as time went on and the number of times traveling this road increased, I noticed another sign about 10 miles from the first.

The second sign read...

FREE FILL DIRT

Not being one who had a great need for fill dirt, I didn't find this sign incredibly relevant to my life situation either.

Keep in mind that my mind always seemed to be on other things.

Not yard signs.

And not on fill dirt.

Plus I am a little thick at times.

So making any sort of connection while driving was unlikely.

Not to mention that I would typically have the music turned up loudly and the windows down with my hair blowing lustrously in the air.

(Yeah whatever)

Needless to say the last thing I was thinking about was a yard sign.

Or how two yard signs could be connected.

But after a couple of months of traveling this road,
And seeing one sign that read *NEED FILL DIRT*
And then seeing the next sign that read *FREE FILL DIRT*

It finally hit me!

I might be the only person in the whole world who could get these two together.

One person needs something and the other has what the first needs.

And here I am.

Right now.

Between the two.

The irony was stunningly beautiful.

_____

That deliberately simple story has cosmic implications.

Implications that shake the very foundations of creation.

And I am not joking about this.

There is a world that desperately needs to discover the riches of the kingdom.

And a God who desperately wants to share and pour out the riches of the kingdom upon each and every person in the world.

The same exact principle holds true.

One needs something and the other has what the first needs.

And guess what?

We might be the only people in the entire world who can get the two together.

Here we are.

Right now.

Between the two.

What will we do about this position in which we find ourselves?

I believe it goes further than just telling one about the other.

Since we are those who are discovering and receiving the kingdom ourselves, we give personal testimony through, not just our words, but with our lives to what God has freely given to us.

We are not just a mouth of the Good News of the kingdom... we are a body to the Good News of the kingdom.

Every thought.
Every word.
Every deed.
Every action.

Everything we have.

Everything we are.

Preaches the Good News of the kingdom.

We are a living, breathing testimony of the kingdom to the world!

And it is that message and that reality that can shake the very foundations of creation.

Not just the singular message of the death, burial, and resurrection of Jesus.

But the entire Good News message of the kingdom!

The sentence AND the exclamation!
The climax AND the resolution!
The reason for which we live AND breathe!

Praise God!

For the truths of this kingdom
that have been hidden
since the beginning of creation,
have been revealed, poured out, and entrusted to us
(the curious, the zealous, and the cynical together)
to bear as a light of righteousness
together, not in opposition,
in the ever-growing darkness of the world
as we await and anticipate the return of the Bridegroom!

AND THEN THE END WILL COME!

_____

NUMBER FOUR!

ONE WITH THEM

Then they will hand you over to suffer affliction and tribulation and put you to death, and you will be hated by all nations for My name's sake. And then many will be offended and repelled and will begin to distrust and desert [Him Whom they ought to trust and obey] and will stumble and fall away and betray one another and pursue one another with hatred. Matthew 24: 9-10

I wear a wristband around my left wrist.

And on this bracelet is written: *One With Them.*

It is a tangible daily reminder for me to pray for Christians who are persecuted around the world.

I found myself struggling to get specific in the prayers, however.

That is until I began to get specific updates from an organization

79

that gives a voice to the voiceless and shares their stories of persecution.

It was then that I began to put names and faces and situations and circumstances together.

And began to pray specifically for them.

One week I prayed for Pastor Benham Irani.

He is locked up in Iran for his faith in Jesus Christ.

He is fighting a blood infection and his health is deteriorating.

Another week I prayed for a retired pastor, Reverend Kabura, and his family.

They lived in Nigeria.

Gunmen came into their home as they were leaving for church services and gunned down the pastor for following Jesus Christ.

Still another week I prayed for Yakubu Kayit and his family.

They lived in Northern Nigeria.

Gunmen came into their home and gunned them down.

And then burned down their home with them in it... because they were followers of Jesus Christ.

And the stories of affliction and persecution for the followers of Christ number in the millions.

Real people.
Real families.
Real lives.
Real relationships.

Crushed.
Broken.
Killed.
Discarded.

Because of their faith and hope in Jesus Christ.

Millions and millions around the globe.
Generation after generation.

They are the faces of affliction and persecution.

_____

And with all of that being said as a backdrop... I am seriously concerned about our American Christian perspective of affliction and persecution.

_____

Which leads to some very important questions.

And it shouldn't surprise you that these questions are all tied to the "End Times."

But even more importantly, they are absolutely essential for our lives today.

When did we, as Christian Americans, get so thin-skinned and so easily offended by everything that people say or do to us?

When did we, as Christian Americans, decide that in the face of opposition, name-calling, and what we call "persecution" that we would begin fighting back rather than counting it, as Jesus would say, "a blessing?"[20]

When did we, as Christian Americans, stop looking to and emulating the way that Jesus lived and the way to which he called his followers, by responding to opposition, name-calling, and "persecution" in humility, submission, and non-retaliation?[21]

When did we, as Christian Americans, replace the best and highest way of "blessing those who curse you" and "praying for those who persecute you," to which Christ called his followers, with crying out like victims?[22]

When did we, as Christian Americans, forget the words of Jesus, "Since they persecuted me, naturally they will persecute you?"[23]

Since they persecuted him.

They will persecute us.

Naturally.

But even in the midst of actions that fall way short of being considered persecution, we get offended, we retaliate, we fight back, and we repay evil for evil.

Think about our track record and the message it sends the world.

We push and fight for the 10 Commandments to be put in front of courthouses.

We cry foul when prayer is not "officially" allowed in schools.

(even though we do not need the approval of anyone to pray I might add)

We push for Creationism to be taught in public schools and get offended when it is struck down within the court system.

And, we put a big fish on our car that is eating a Darwin creature to make the not-so-subtle point that we will triumph.

Ugh.

Our fighting.
Our retaliating.
Our pettiness.

They compromise the kingdom.
They are counter-productive to the reign of God.

Yeah.

In response to things that *should not* even be considered in the same league as persecution.

They may be inconveniences.
They may be frustrations.
They may not be what you personally like or want.

But they can't be considered persecution.

And we are certainly not afflicted.

Even though we think that we are.

Here is the truth when it comes to this stuff.

We do not like to take the low and humble way of Jesus by picking up the towel to wash the feet of our enemies.

But that is the kingdom we are called to preach and embody to the nations.

We do not like practicing the way of turning the other cheek when someone strikes us.

But that is the kingdom we are called to preach and embody to the nations.

We do not like forgiving those who have trespassed against us.

But that is the kingdom we are called to preach and embody to the nations.

We do not like blessing others when they ridicule, mock, antagonize, or treat us unkindly.

Repeat after me.

Together.

But that is the kingdom we are called to preach and embody to the nations.

It is no wonder we only want to preach a small sliver of the Good News, because the rest of the Good News makes us too uncomfortable.

_____

Instead of preaching and embodying the Good News of the kingdom, we respond the way the rest of the world responds.

Which is very different than the way of Jesus and the way to which he calls his followers.

Rather than being a people who are meek, or overly submissive, we fight and claw to defend ourselves and to defend Christ.

(who, by the way, does not need to be defended)

Rather than taking the road of the suffering-servant, we rise above to crush or silence the opposition.

Rather than being the poor in spirit, we form coalitions and advocacy groups and political action groups to be mighty in power.

Rather than blessing everyone in the world with our words of life and love, we choose to curse those whom we believe are against us.

Rather than being peacemakers by not participating in the endless cycle of retaliation and fighting and war, we extend and perpetuate the conflict.

Rather than looking like the embodiment of Christ through our self-sacrificial love to friend and enemy alike, we respond in anger, frustration, and sometimes even hatred.

The way of the kingdom captivates a world through love.

Anything done in our own power repels the world in antagonism.

_____

Let this story serve as an example.

One Sunday.

We showed up at our rented church building.

Someone had spray painted a Nazi swastika on the front of the building.

We didn't pay much attention to it as it looked like the work of some foolish children.

But after a couple of weeks the swastika was still there.

I heard some people in our church musing over an idea to use spray paint to turn the swastika into a cross.

I didn't pay much attention to the idea.

I thought everyone was just having fun with ways to "redeem" a terrible symbol.

I didn't think they were serious.

However, a few days later I was riding my bike passed our building, I noticed that, sure enough, the swastika had been transformed into a cross.

With the word "love" written beside it.

I didn't say anything about it.

But I did not like what had been done.

As I anticipated, my fears came to fruition.

I returned back to the building later in the week to find that the word "NAZI" had been spray-painted on the building again.

And this time.

Along.

The.

Entire.

Front.

Of.

The.

Building.

Including the windows.

This was retaliation for our naive move.

Lesson learned.

Violence begets more violence.

Even when it is just spray paint.

_____

Here's the point.

When we respond to people in the same way they treat us... the vicious cycle begins.

One group tries to rise above the other group.

Tit-for-tat.

Eye for eye.

Tooth for tooth.

Retaliating.
Responding.
Escalating.

This approach creates more hostility and divisiveness and antagonism and conflict.

This approach NEVER changes hearts.

It may change behavior for a bit.

But it NEVER changes hearts.

It just embitters and callouses and hardens and begs for retaliation.

The cycle never ends.

Unless someone stops the cycle.

And that someone has to be us.

The followers of Christ.

The proclaimers and extenders of the kingdom.

Our way must be the lowly and humble and meek and loving and blessed and non-retaliating approach of our Christ.

Our way must be the way of Christ, the peacemaker.

No other way will do.

Because when one submits in love… the cycle stops.

That's the way of Jesus.

And it has to be our way as well.

It is only the way of Jesus and the kingdom that changes hearts and changes minds.

And it is that way that will eventually change the world.

———

But that is the true dilemma.

How will we ever respond to *real affliction and persecution* in the way of Jesus and his kingdom… if we neglect the way of Jesus and his kingdom when other people simply inconvenience us or frustrate us?

How will we ever love someone who beats us and is trying to crush us… when we don't even love those who simply make fun of Christianity with their words?

How will we ever bless someone who imprisons us… when we don't even bless the atheist who says God doesn't exist?

How will we ever humbly and lovingly serve someone who takes everything from us… when we don't even serve those who try to remove "In God We Trust" from our currency, who try to remove the Ten Commandments from public property, who keep Creationism out of the public school system, or who try to keep prayer out of school?

How will we ever say "Father forgive them" about someone who kills our loved ones… when we don't even ask God to forgive someone who paints our church building or who steals something belonging to our church?

How will we ever be entrusted and given more of this kingdom to extend… if we can't even be trusted with a little?

The truth is that we have a lot of kingdom to discover and embody before we will ever be prepared for anything that resembles the "End Times."

For if we are not like Jesus when times are relatively easy, there is no way we will ever be like him if our lives grow increasingly difficult and hostile.

———

I believe that is why Jesus says that so many people will stumble and fall away and betray one another.

Because we will have never known or will have already abandoned the kingdom.

To many…

Christianity will have just been a civic religion.
And they will abandon it when times get tough.

Christianity will have just been a nice thing to take the kids to on Sundays.
And they will abandon it when times get tough.

Christianity will have just been a good group to associate with.
And they will abandon it when times get tough.

Christianity will have just been a means to be entertained.
And they will abandon it when times get tough.

Man, I hate to be such a Debbie Downer in this chapter.

But if we really want to be honest about what Jesus said
And not just focus on the war and earthquake talk,

Then we have to realize that he said many would abandon the faith when times get tough.

Let's get real.
If economies collapse and lawlessness rules and resources are scarce, many people who claim with their mouths that they follow Jesus... will abandon him with their lives.
Life will be more about self-preservation... than extending the kingdom.

Life will be more about taking care of our own needs... than extending the kingdom.

Life will be more about staying alive... than extending the kingdom.

Life will be more about hoarding... than extending the kingdom.

Life will be more about protection... than extending the kingdom.

Life will be more about retaliation... than extending the kingdom.

Life will be more about division… than extending the kingdom.

Life will be more about hatred… than extending the kingdom.

Life will be more about fear… than extending the kingdom.

Life will be more about worry… than extending the kingdom.

Life will be more about anxiety… than extending the kingdom.

Life will be more about tears… than extending the kingdom.

And that is what will be the greatest sadness on earth.

If the light of the world goes dark.

If those who are to carry the light of righteousness and hope abandon it.

If the light that should remain burning until the return of the bridegroom burns out.

_____

I can't underscore how important it is for our light to burn brightly in the darkness.

In a world growing increasingly hard and cold and bitter and unloving.

The world needs the bright light of love and kindness and service and hope.

It matters in the lives of real people.

Who ache.
Who hurt.
Who feel dejected.

Who feel like there is nowhere to turn.
Who feel scared and utterly alone.
Who feel like giving up.
Who feel like taking their own lives.

It matters right now.
And it will continue to matter even more in the future.

_____

One day I met a guy who was homeless.

He didn't meet any of the criteria to get into the local homeless shelter.

And he had nowhere to go.

I told him that he could stay in the upstairs of our church building until he figured out something else.

On his first night I thought I would stop by to check on him to see if he needed anything.

When I walked up the stairs and entered the main room I could hear two people talking.

A man.
A woman.

What did I get myself into?

They walked out of the back room together and around the corner.

When they saw me the guy told the lady, "This is just the guy you need to talk to."

I was somewhat confused and perplexed.

But the lady walked toward me and asked if we could talk.

We sat down at the table and she began to tell me her story.

She explained how she always walked by our building.

But was always too afraid to come in.

With tears in her eyes she told me about her life and her children.

And her meth addiction.

I listened.

And cried with her.

She asked if I would pray over her.

And I did.

I prayed with every ounce of the Spirit in my heart.

And with tears streaming down my face.

As we left the building I asked if I could get her phone number so I could keep in touch with her and possibly help her get checked into a treatment center.

She gave it to me.

———

I called the next day and spoke with her.

She sounded interested in treatment.

I told her I would get everything arranged.

When I tried to call her a few days later... the number was disconnected.

_____

I was so devastated and sad.

So many questions.

Where did she go?
What about her kids?
Did things get worse?
Did she give up?
Was life too much?

There was a weight in my heart that I believed would never be resolved.

So I did the only thing I knew I could do.

I prayed for her everyday.

I knew her name.

And I made sure that God knew it as well.

She was a constant fixture in my mind.

God please protect her and let her know that she is loved and she is valuable.

Let her know that there is a light in the darkness.

Let her know that there is still so much life to be lived.

_____

I remember the day vividly.

It was a Sunday.

The sun was brilliantly shining on that spring morning.

And it was an absolutely glorious morning as we gathered together as a church.

After I finished teaching that day I saw a lady leaving the building who looked vaguely familiar.

Could it have been her?

I started to ask around.

Hey, does anyone know the name of the lady who just left?

My buddy answered.

It was her.

And, to my surprise and delight, she same back the next Sunday.

I went up to her and asked if she remembered me.

She gave me the biggest hug ever.

And then told me that after we met together... she started to get clean.

She got off the meth.

She asked God to be an active part of her life.

She got her kids back.

She got a job.

And she has been clean for over a year and a half.

Praise God.

Just the other day she sent this note to me...

You have been an inspiration to me more then you will ever know.
I know I have told you how blessed I was to have God send you
to my rescue that evening and I know if it wasn't for you and that
gentleman that day I wouldn't be here to see my children grow. God
bless you.

_____

As I sit here writing I am thinking about the last 72 hours.

And how important everything I have talked about in this chapter
really is.

Because beyond the text is real life.

It's more than words.
It's more than metaphors.
It's more than poetic language.
It's more than lofty ideas.
It's more than idealistic thinking.
It's more than a nice sentiment.
It's more than a pep talk.

It's flesh and blood and life and death.

And it all teeters on a thin precipice.

It's incredibly fragile.

And the words we use mean everything.
And the ways we treat people mean everything.
And the care we shower over people means everything.

And the love, the love we envelop people with means everything.

_____

I got a text that said I needed to call a friend of mine immediately, because she was about to do something drastic.

Nervously, I began to text my friend.

One text after another text after another.

Are you ok?

Hey, it's Brandon.

If you want to talk, please call me.

No response.

I was very concerned and started praying for her.

Finally after about ten minutes... she called.

I wasn't quite sure what was in store for me.

But as we inched our way through pleasantries (which didn't feel very pleasant)...

My.

Heart.

Just.

Sank.

On Christmas Day my friend tried to take her life.

With those words alone... tears began filling my eyes.

But it even got worse.

She told me that she was going to try it again.

Because she had lost all hope.

She said that she was spoiling her marriage.
She said that she was spoiling her relationship with her son.
She said that she was spoiling everything around her.

She felt alone and empty.
Inconsequential.
With no purpose.
With no reason to live another day.

_____

I don't know if you have ever spoken to a person who has lost all hope.

But if you ever do... it will change you forever.

You will never want another person in your life to ever feel that way.

The ache is too much to bear.

But it will also teach you how completely powerless you are to say or do anything to help.

You feel out of your league.
Like you aren't equipped.
Like you don't have the skills or the words.

You feel as if there is nothing you can do.
Because the situation feels too powerful and overwhelming.

And you realize.
In all of your weakness and humility.
How desperately you need God to help you.

I was praying so hard for God to help me and give me the words that I couldn't seem to find on my own.

Words to help my friend see her beauty and purpose and reason to live.

And then God began to speak through my words.

Even if you can't see it yourself right now, the reason I am here, the reason I exist, the reason I am talking to you on the phone is to tell you that you do matter. You do have a purpose. You are loved.

And if you don't believe it matters to anyone else if you are alive... will you at least choose to stay alive because it matters to me?... and I believe in you... I believe in you, my friend.

Praise God that she chose to live another day.

———

Three days later.

After the story above.

My good friend Kim, who is staying with my family while she is on sabbatical from her mission work in New Zealand, walked in our front door and said, "I have had the craziest day ever."

If you knew my friend Kim, you would stop cold in your tracks if you heard her say that she had the craziest day ever.

Because she has...

An absolutely, positively crazy life.

She said to my wife and I... *You know how I was supposed to go to the north side of Indy today?*

Well, I never made it.

I have been hanging out with a lesbian prostitute and a dude who is a junkie.

Ok.

Curious to know how Kim's plans changed so dramatically, we listened intently.

Kim had to make a pit stop at Target.

She had a few things to pick up.

As she drove through the parking lot in her borrowed soccer mom van, a man ran up to her window and asked her if she had some jumper cables.

Fortunately she did.

She pulled up next to his car and got out of the soccer mom van.

The only problem is that Kim had no idea how to use jumper cables.
And after about ten minutes, Kim didn't know if the man or the other lady he was with knew how to use them either.
The problem wasn't the battery... it was the starter of the car.

The man thanked Kim for her time and told her to have a good day.

My guess is that most people would have been content with simply offering to help.

But Kim isn't most people.

She offered to buy him a cup of coffee in the store.

In a moment that could only have been understood as divine...

He said he would join her inside for the coffee.

————

As they sat down for coffee, he asked Kim where she was from.

She said Indiana.

But then she told him that she was also a missionary in New Zealand.

That is when things got really wild.

He said, "So you are like God."

Kim, a little wigged out by the assertion, said, "Ok, that's cool."

And then he said, "No, like I have been praying to God because my wife just left me and I have been depressed and I have been trying to kill myself by cutting my wrists."

That's when he pulled up his sleeves.

Kim knew at that point that she was completely out of her league.

So she started to pray that she would have the right words.

He went on to tell her about his prison time and how much he had screwed up his marriage and how he steals Furbies and then returns them for store gift cards.

It was then that he shared with Kim that he believed his car broke down for a reason... and that God had sent Kim to talk to him.

_____

He went back out to the car and began to work on it again while Kim picked up a few things in the store.

When she met up with them again in the parking lot... she offered them a ride.

The man and woman talked a bit and agreed to the offer.

But he didn't really know where he could go because his wife had recently kicked him out of their house.

And he had burned too many bridges with his parents to go to their house.

So the lady, who had just been cussing someone out on her phone, gave Kim an address of where to take her.

Upon arrival, Kim realized that the destination was where this lady's next customer lived.

Not to be dissuaded, Kim waited in her car with her new friend and began to listen to his story again about depression and suicide and how God sent her to him.

And she listened.
And she listened.
And she listened.

And prayed for the right words.

Kim told the man that she knew what it was like to be depressed and to be in a downward spiral and to want to end it all.

But she also told him that she had found hope in Jesus… and it was that hope that had given her a reason to live.

Their lady friend came back from a quick job.

They loaded up and took off once more.

This time dropping her off at her final destination.

Kim and her guy friend continued on to McDonald's where Kim offered to buy him a meal.

He kept telling her that he could not understand why she was being so nice.

She talked to him for two more hours.

He told her how much he wanted to be off drugs and how he wanted to have a purpose and how he wanted to stop stealing Furbies.

Kim told him that there wasn't anything she could say that would change his heart.

She knew this from experience.

The only thing that could change him, and it was the same thing that had changed her, was God breaking into the darkness of his heart and completely changing him and restoring him.

Only Christ could change his heart and his life.

That is when he wept.

He said that even though he had not been in contact with his parents in five days, and that his mom had filed a missing person's request on him, he needed to go to their house.

But he was really afraid to face up to his life and was really afraid to make changes.

Kim took this 34-year-old broken man to his parent's house and walked him to the door.

She gave him a note with her phone number on it and told him to call her if he ever felt like giving up again.

Even if you feel like no one else cares about you. I do.

With tears in his eyes he responded to Kim by saying, "Meeting you is like God giving me one more chance to get my life cleaned up."

––––––

If people feel lost and alone and helpless and broken and hopeless today, what will it be like if the world really begins to come apart at the hinges?

What will it be like for those who are already hanging by a thread?

Who will be there with words of life and encouragement?
Who will be there with a shoulder on which to cry?
Who will be there to give them hope for another day?
Who will be there to tell them that they matter?
Who will be there to reassure them that they are loved?
Who will be there to say, "I believe in you."?
Who will be there to tell them that God has a purpose for their lives?

If we are more concerned about saving our own skin...
If we are more concerned about taking care of our own needs...
If we are more concerned about staying alive...

If we are more concerned about hoarding for ourselves...
If we are more concerned about our protection...
If we are more concerned about retaliation...
If we are more concerned about dividing and staying away from people...
If we are more concerned about hating others...
If we are more concerned about our own fears...
If we are more concerned about our own worries...
If we are more concerned about our own anxieties...
If we are more concerned more about our own tears...
If we are more concerned about all of those things...

And we run and abandon Jesus and the kingdom when it gets tough for us...

Then how will people ever be able to see the light of Christ and find hope?

The truth of the matter is that we exist for a purpose.

Today.

And tomorrow.

And forever.

Everything single thing we do has eternal impact.

The way we love.
The way we encourage.
The way we serve.
The way we share a meal.
The way we embrace.
The way we give all we have.
The way we live our lives.

It all matters.

It matters for our own sake.

It matters for the sake of the kingdom.

And it matters to every single person who is losing hope and who begins to lose hope in the future.

Believe me.

This is what my friend wrote to me yesterday after our conversation:

Thank you for caring and believing in me. I love your spirit and trust in you so much. You are the only person I would have listened to right then. Your prayers are what have gotten me this far. Thank you B. You are a great man.

To God be the glory, for using us to shine his Light in this world in both good times and bad.

———

NUMBER FIVE!

IF MOMMA AIN'T HAPPY

Watch out that no one deceives you. For many will come in my name, claiming, 'I am the Messiah,' and will deceive many. Matthew 24: 4-5

I want to speak from personal experience here.

If you are married, you will know what I am talking about.

If you are single, you would be wise to take notes.

I am the stereotypical man.

When I am locked into something and I have all of my concentration directed to it... you would be lucky to get my attention.

For the few who have been so lucky to redirect my attention away from whatever it is I am reading, writing, or watching...

They may get eye contact.

But they do not get my full attention.

Especially when I am writing.

My eyes are glued to the computer monitor.

My ear buds are planted deeply within my aural cavity.

The volume is turned up loudly enough to block all outside noise, including voices.

(and even if I hear a voice... I pretend I don't hear it)

I am in the zone.

And hopefully Jenny doesn't read this chapter.

Just kidding.

_____

But I am not bragging about this!

This is truly a confession.

I promise.

However, my wife has gotten really, really good at catching me when I do this.

She just knows.

She won't walk over and try to get my attention.

She won't wave her arms so I will look at her.
She won't even raise her voice in hopes that I will take out the ear buds.

Nope.

She just says it one more time at the same volume.

That's it.

So when she asks me to change Will's diaper the first time, but still doesn't have my attention...

I can assure you that when she says it for the second time...

I better be standing up and moving toward Will's nuclear deposit.

Because if momma ain't happy.

Ain't nobody happy.

_____

Of course I am embellishing a bit for dramatic effect.

My wife is awesome.

When she asks me to do something or gives me instruction about something, I want to do it because I love her.

And I always try to do it the first time.

But I can be incredibly obtuse and incoherent at times.

So unfortunately she does have to ask or give instruction a second time.

And to be honest, when she has to tell me something a second time... I am actually a little embarrassed.

When you love someone, you want to give that person respect by listening and taking what he or she says to heart.

Especially if it is something that is really important.

———

And I don't know if you noticed this earlier,

But during Jesus' war and earthquake "End Times" speech,

He said something really important.

Okay, okay, everything he said was important.

But this was so important that he repeated it.

Watch out that no one deceives you. For many will come in my name, claiming, 'I am the Messiah,' and will deceive many.

And then he said it again.

This time offering even more detail and caution.

At that time if anyone says to you, 'Look, here is the Messiah!' or, 'There he is!' do not believe it.

For false messiahs and false prophets will appear and perform great signs and wonders to deceive, if possible, even the elect.

See, I have told you ahead of time.

He then adds...

So if anyone tells you, 'There he is, out in the wilderness,' do not go out; or, 'Here he is, in the inner rooms,' do not believe it.

For as lightning that comes from the east is visible even in the west, so will be the coming of the Son of Man.

Wherever there is a carcass, there the vultures will gather.

———

To me, man...

Jesus repeating himself

is a big deal.

A very big deal.

He's like.

Hey disciples... if you somehow missed this important warning at the beginning ... then... boom!

Here it comes again!

Don't miss it this time!

If Jenny tells me something important two times within two minutes, it means that she really wants me to remember it.

Sure I might miss it the first time.

But it doesn't take more than two times for me to know that she means it.

And because I love her, I listen and take it to heart.

That is how the disciples were.

I am sure of it.

They loved their friend with all of their hearts.

When he spoke, they listened.

They didn't always get everything right… but they listened to him and wanted to honor him with their lives.

And there is no doubt in my mind that by the time Jesus mentioned it again, they heard every single word of his important warning.

_____

Here is my simpleton summary of Jesus' important warning:

Watch out!
There will be people who try to deceive you.
There will be people who try to lead you astray.
Some will even claim to be the Messiah.
And they will be very convincing.
Large crowds will gather to get in on the action.
So be careful and be wary of charismatic leaders with mass appeal.

_____

I have to be really honest.

These words of warning from Jesus significantly bother me.

Yeah.

They bother me more than anything else he said.

Even more than the earthquakes and wars stuff.

No joke.

Not because I disagree with him.

Not because I am always looking around the corner for another Anti-Christ boogeyman.

Not because it scares me or stresses me out.

But because he says that many will be led astray.

And.
That.
Completely.
Breaks.
My.
Heart.

BIG.
TIME.

Not in an I-know-I-ought-to-feel-bad-because-I-am-writing-a-book-kinda-way… but in a serious-heavy-hearted-kinda-way.

That's why this warning really bothers me.

———

For any person to be led astray means that he or she must have been on the right track at one point.

In other words.

There are, and have been, many people who say they follow Christ.

But some have already been, and some will continue to be, led away from Christ.

And the reason I am making such a massive deal about this is because...

If a person is led astray from Christ... then does anything else that Jesus said in his "End Times" speech even matter?

That is why this chapter may be the most important.

Because you very well may be one of the people Jesus is talking about.

You may be the fair-weather follower who is easily led astray.

So please take all of these words to heart.

_____

There may be those who read these warnings of Jesus and discount them.

They may say:

All of that stuff is historical and it already happened... so give it a rest.

-or-

That stuff may happen some time in the future but it really isn't important today.

And you know what?

I get it.

Believe me.

I get both arguments.

I understand that there are different perspectives about this stuff.

In fact, I have read every single "End Times" perspective that is out there.

But here is the thing.

The larger idea
the larger principle
of what Jesus is getting after
(which is: *don't be deceived and led astray*)
is way more important than the *when-is-this-stuff-gonna-happen* or *has-this-stuff-already-happened* debate.

And if we make a commitment to understand the bigger picture of what Jesus is saying, then whether the "End Times"…

has happened in the past
or is happening right now
or will be happening in the future

is completely inconsequential.

That's right.

All of those theories are completely inconsequential.

Not being deceived and not being led astray is way more important right now.

Don't forget it.

And it always has been and will always continue to be important.

Trying to figure out *when* is never more important than the warning itself.

Comprende'?

So whether you are a part of this debate or not,
It does not matter.

If you are… then here's a good idea.

Let's get focused on what's really important.

If you aren't… then here's a really good idea.

Let's get focused on what's really important.

Either way, it is a good idea for all of us to come together and focus on what is really important.

And that is – *to know Jesus so well that we never stray from him.*

It is *always a good idea* to know Jesus Christ and to know him so thoroughly and to know him so intimately that there is absolutely no way anyone could ever lead us astray.

And that is where I have landed on this issue.

To me… whether the "End Times" happened in the past or is happening right now or may happen in the future… it is completely irrelevant to me.

It just does not matter.

Because.

If knowing Jesus Christ and his kingdom is my central pursuit
If knowing Jesus Christ and his kingdom is my central obsession
If knowing Jesus Christ and his kingdom is my life goal

Then there is no conceivable way I will ever be led astray by anyone.

Ever.

EVER.

Whether it is the "End Times" or not.

_____

But the key is to give everything we have and everything we are...

To knowing Jesus intimately
To knowing his kingdom thoroughly
To knowing his voice specifically

And staying close to him... period.

For that is where our true protection and security in this life is found.

_____

In the Gospel of John.

Jesus said those who stay close to him are like sheep.[24]

Sheep who hear him.

Sheep who listen to his voice.

We hear him.
We know his voice.
It is familiar to each of us.

And he said that when we stay close to him
He gives us eternal life that we will never lose throughout the ages.

And he said that when we stay close to him

No one is able to snatch us away from his protection.

This should give us the courage and the certainty that we are safe at all times when we stay close to Jesus and remain close to his familiar voice.

Jesus is more than sufficient for us.
Jesus is more than enough for us.
Jesus is all we need.

We do not need to put our hope, faith, or reliance in anyone or anything else.

We do not need to put our hope, faith, and reliance in leaders.

We do not need to put our hope, faith, and reliance in our government.

We do not need to put our hope, faith, and reliance in our country.

We do not need to put our hope, faith, and reliance in our economic system.

We do not need to put our hope, faith, and reliance in structures or institutions.

Our hope, faith, and reliance in Jesus is all we need.

For it is Jesus alone who can give us real and meaningful life.

So make a commitment in your life to ONLY know Jesus and his kingdom.

Nothing else.

No one else.

That is the most essential piece of advice that anyone could ever
give you to never be led astray.

_____

It seems as if everything I have said in this chapter was building
toward this.

And this is what concerns me the most.

In the United States
We are collectively so far from the shepherd's voice
That we are precariously susceptible to other voices.

And when we have strayed from the voice of the Shepherd
And when we have strayed from the only one who can offer us
protection and real, meaningful life

And when our daily lives are disrupted or turned upside-down
Or when a crisis or catastrophe occurs

We run to other voices because we are afraid.
And they sound so good and so promising.

Yet in the process we abandon the one who really loves us and cares
for us and wants the best for us.

_____

That is why staying close to Jesus
And not straying
Is so important.

Because in the midst of chaos or confusion
Or in the throes of economic upheaval
Or in the face of a shortage of food
Or any other crisis

There will be people who appeal to your fear and who offer protection.

There will be people who will appeal to your uncertainty and who offer certainty.

There will be people who will appeal to your insecurity and who offer security.

There will be people who will appeal to your worry and who offer their confidence.

There will be people who will appeal to your hunger and who offer food.

There will be people who will appeal to your lack and who offer plenty.

But in return they will ask...

For your allegiance.
For your trust.
For your confidence.
For your pledge.

And while all of these things make perfect sense, according to worldly wisdom, in order to get by another day,

Giving our allegiance and trust and confidence and pledge to anyone but Jesus Christ as Lord and to his kingdom is exactly what we have been warned against.

Because the ways of those who lead us astray
Are diametrically opposed to the ways of Jesus.

They are ways that lead to death, not life.
They are ways that lead to division, not unity.
They are ways that lead to retaliation, not peace.

They are ways that lead to injustice, not mercy.
They are ways that lead to power, not humility.
They are ways that lead away from God, not toward.

That is the danger.

And we should be very cautious about giving our allegiance, trust,
confidence, or pledge to any group or person that unites people around
death, division, retaliation, injustice, power, and godlessness.

Today or in the future.

_____

And again, this sounds quite a bit like our country.

We have a lot of leaders and politicians and religious leaders calling
us toward

Their vision.
Their values.
Their principles.
Their world-view.
Their methods.
Their tactics.

They try to sell us things all the time that we don't need.

But we buy it.

Like sheep that have been led astray,
We aimlessly follow.

Even though.

Their ways look like division.
Their ways look like opposition.
Their ways look like enemy lists.

Their ways look like indebtedness.
Their ways look like name-calling.
Their ways look like fighting back.
Their ways look like slander.
Their ways look like aggression.
Their ways look like hostility.
Their ways look like oppression.
Their ways look like war.
Their ways look like subversion.
Their ways look like idolatry.
Their ways look like self-preservation.
Their ways look like back door deals.
Their ways look like self-promotion.
Their ways look like devaluing life.
Their ways look like double-talk and lying.
Their ways look like death.

And those ways look nothing like Jesus and his kingdom.

But we listen to their voices.
And we follow.
And give them our support.
And give them our allegiance.

And we begin to act like them.
And we begin to talk like them.
And we begin to take on their values.
And we begin to take on their principles.
And we begin to treat others like they treat people.
And we begin to fight on their behalf.

So again, be mindful of the leaders and the groups with whom you are aligning.

And in whom you place your hope.
And in whom you place your faith.
And in whom you place your trust.

And be aware of the leaders and the groups to whom you give your pledge.

And to whom you give your allegiance.
And to whom you give your promise.
And to whom you give your time.
And to whom you give your effort.
And to whom you give your heart.

Because the raw and essential truth is that if *anyone or anything* deviates from Jesus in any way, shape, or form...

It leads us astray.

And it takes us from him.

And it takes us from his kingdom way.

And it takes us from his voice and his protection and his eternal life.

It is just that plain and simple.

And it is what we ought to be guarding against at all times.

––––––––––

When we stay close to Jesus and we know his kingdom, the world can be turned completely upside-down, yet we will remain consistently his, and will uncompromisingly continue in his way.

When we stay close to Jesus and we know his kingdom, the political parties and ideological groups can scratch and claw and lie and spend and cheat, yet we will remain consistently his, and will uncompromisingly continue in his way.

When we stay close to Jesus and we know his kingdom, a president can make policies that we completely disagree with, yet we will remain consistently his, and will uncompromisingly continue in his way.

When we stay close to Jesus and we know his kingdom, our country can begin to fall to pieces, yet we will remain consistently his, and will uncompromisingly continue in his way.

When we stay close to Jesus and we know his kingdom, our economy can fall apart and our money can be made worthless, yet we will remain consistently his, and will uncompromisingly continue in his way.

When we stay close to Jesus and we know his kingdom, news media can try to use propaganda to manipulate us, yet we will remain consistently his, and will uncompromisingly continue in his way.

When we stay close to Jesus and we know his kingdom, we can be mocked, scorned, laughed at, beaten, and threatened, yet we will remain consistently his, and will uncompromisingly continue in his way.

When we stay close to Jesus and we know his kingdom, the vultures can circle and congregate where death is found, yet we will remain consistently his, and will uncompromisingly continue in his way.

When we stay close to Jesus and we know his kingdom, our churches can be burned to the ground and we can be run out of town, yet we will remain consistently his, and will uncompromisingly continue in his way.

Because he has our pledge and our promise and our allegiance… that we will never leave him or forsake him.

We will never wander or go astray.

We will never be deceived by anyone no matter how convincing they may be.

And he does not need to give us this warning twice.

Because we heard him the first time.

And we will do what he says with all of our hearts because we love him.

——

CONCLUSION!

Anyone who knows me also knows that it is impossible for me to have a conversation without coffee coming up at some point in the conversation.

Writing a book without mentioning coffee, well, that would be a high crime.

I frequently visit my friendly neighborhood Starbucks, which I also refer to as "my office."

And man... I love those people.

Pam.
Bucky.
Peter T.
Kelly.
Nina.
Anita.

And the rest of the gang.

Good stuff.

I love stopping by and hanging out.

And I do frequently.

The funny thing about this particular Starbucks is that it has a Fitness Center connected to it.

No, silly, Starbucks didn't start their own Fitness Center.

The two businesses occupy space within the same larger building.

I didn't think too much about how funny that actually was... until I was sitting at a table sipping some brew and started to "people watch."

Don't jump to any conclusions here.

I don't "people watch" to judge anyone.

In fact, I find myself regularly praying for people I see.

But on this particular day, I had to laugh.

An intentionally non-descript person in full fitness workout gear with sweat dripping from his or her forehead walked into the store and began to place his or her order.

Venti.
Mocha-something.
Whole milk.
Double Whip.
Chocolate drizzle.

With a chocolate-covered Biscotti dunked deep within the drink.

It was some drink (or dessert).

And there is no way it could have been less than a 1000 calories.

I am sure it could have sufficed as an entire meal or two.

To be fair here, Starbucks does have low-calorie options.

I think my black coffee has like 5 calories.

And I said that to stay out of hot water.

But seriously.

Fitness workout gear, sweat on the brow, and a 1000-calorie dessert drink!

The irony.

_____

I like that story a lot.

And I don't bring it up to demean anyone or to criticize a person's eating habits.

I think it is a funny story.

I bring it up because it is a perfect representation of many Christians.

Including me.

Which also tells me how far we have yet to go.

We metaphorically clothe ourselves in the fitness workout gear of Jesus Christ… signifying our new identity and good intentions.

We may even put our new identity and good intentions to use occasionally and work up a sweat.

But at the end of the day,

even though we have clothed ourselves in something new,

and even though we tell the world of our good intentions to change and live a completely new life,

and even though we go through the motions of what we think we ought to be doing,

the truth is that we have not really been completely changed from the inside-out.

We still fall back to the old 1000-calorie ways of our old selves that got us in this mess in the first place.

Because that is the place where life is easy.
Because that is the place where life is comfortable.
Because that is the place where we can avoid risk.
Because that is the place where we can avoid pain.
Because that is the place where very little is expected of me.

And because that is the place where sacrifice is not needed.

———

I think it is interesting that there was a point in Jesus' ministry when larger crowds began to follow him around, but rather than let them continue to follow him like a rock star or a celebrity... he turned and faced them and made sure they understood the cost of following him.

It doesn't cost anything to simply follow me.

It doesn't cost anything to simply walk around behind me.

It doesn't cost anything to simply listen to my message.

And that is what Jesus wanted to make sure all of the groupies understood.

There is a cost to following me... and it is your whole life.

If any of you come to me and do not hate your father and mother and wife and children and brothers and sisters and, yes, even your own life...

You cannot be my disciple.[25]

And.

That.

Has.

A.

Way.

Of.

Thinning.

Out.

The.

Crowd.

Hard core Jesus.

I am telling you.

In my 38-years of church.

I have.

NEVER.

EVER.

Heard a preacher preach on those words of Jesus.
They are just too controversial.

But let me offer some perspective, before you begin to wig out and think Jesus is telling us to hate the people we love.

Because he is not.

_____

Here is what he is saying.

In comparison to the attitude and disposition and over-the-top affinity, love, and adoration that we have toward God...

any relationship...

including those whom we love the most and to whom we are the closest...

will look like relative disregard or hatred.

We don't truly hate them.

That would be counter-intuitive to the entire ministry and message of Jesus.

More specifically.

Jesus is saying that...

our love
our commitment

our devotion to God
is so crazy
and so extreme
and so over the top
that *everything* else
pales in comparison.

So unless we are willing to sacrifice everything, even those closest to us, we are not fit to be his disciples.

Tough stuff.

But he went even further.

If we are not willing to follow his example and deny ourselves and pick up our crosses, we are not fit to be his disciples.[26]

If we are not willing to follow his example and lay down our lives in order to demonstrate the expansive breadth and the immeasurable depth of God's love for others, we are not fit to be his disciples.

If we are not willing to follow his example and give up everything that we believe is essential to our lives, we are not fit to be his disciples.

Jesus isn't being hardcore for the sake of being hardcore.

He is being honest about what it will take to find real life.

A life fully surrendered to God.

Follow me because I am all you need.

I am the Way, the Truth, the Life.[27]

Who would not give up everything for that?

In Jesus.

A real Life.
A meaningful Life.
A hopeful Life.
An abundant Life.
A free Life.
A full Life.

Is not just a possibility.

It is a reality.

Boom.

_____

But there are few who find the reality of that Life.

The gate to that Life is very narrow.

And the road leading there is hard to follow.

Going to church does not guarantee Life.
Saying the name of Jesus does not guarantee Life.
Reciting the sinner's prayer does not guarantee Life.
Getting baptized does not guarantee Life.
Doing something nice for someone does not guarantee Life.

That is why Jesus drew a hard line in the sand with the crowd.

Because true Life is only found by fully receiving the love of God and totally surrendering everything to Him.

And one would rather die than to ever stop living in that kind of all-consuming, enveloping, and overwhelming love.

_____

And my guess is that most of you agree with all of that.

At least in theory.

Of course we love God with all of our hearts, minds, and souls!

Of course we would rather die than to ever stop living in that kind of all-consuming, enveloping, and overwhelming love!

I hear you.

But here's the kicker.

It doesn't stop there.

This all-consuming, enveloping, and overwhelming love is not simply meant to be received.

It is meant to be *given* as well.

And here is what that means.

It means that we would rather die than to ever stop *giving* that kind of all-consuming, enveloping, and overwhelming love.

What is received… is to be *given*.

And that turns everything completely upside-down.

———

Perfect love casts away all fear.

If we receive perfect love.

If we give perfect love.

There is nothing to fear.

But fear has a massive death grip on us.

We are afraid of instability.
We are afraid of tyranny.
We are afraid of "losing freedom."
We are afraid of opposing ideologies.
We are afraid of the government.
We are afraid of "losing our rights."
We are afraid of the government "taking our guns."
We are afraid of the government taking our religious liberties.
We are afraid of our money becoming worthless.
We are afraid of losing our jobs.
We are afraid of "new world orders."
We are afraid of Anti-Christ figures.

Don't miss what I am saying here.

I am *not* saying that we ought not work peacefully and prayerfully to oppose those things that work against the extension of the kingdom of God in the world.

But what I am saying is that as we receive perfect love from God... we begin to realize that we have absolutely nothing to fear.

And as we give that perfect love to others... we fear nothing.

Everything else fades away.

Only perfect love remains.

And it is exquisite and beautiful.

If we would really open ourselves up to experience that kind of love, we would have no other choice than to believe that it is worth living in, giving to others, and dying for.

Because it is a better narrative.
Because it subverts the conflict.

Because it was the way we were always made to live.
Because that is what God intended for us at the very beginning.

And it is with that kind of perfect love that this life is to be lived and experienced.

Not by avoiding the conflict.
Not by praying for a "Rapture" of the church every moment.
Not by constantly begging Jesus to return and take you away to heaven.

But by gracefully and mercifully and lovingly and prayerfully walking through the conflict and chaos of life, while working toward and anticipating resolution.

The way we choose to live presently is a good indication of how we will choose to live in the future.

That is why we need to change right now.

_____

By this point you have probably picked up on the true "End Times" theme of this book.

If we aren't living like Christ presently, when times are relatively good, then we will never live like Christ if times get really difficult in the future.

And it is no different in this chapter.

But this chapter may be harder to swallow than the others.

_____

It's harder to swallow because it confronts us with how insufficient and negligent we have been at extending the all-consuming, enveloping, and overwhelming love of God.

Think about it.

Are you criticizing, demeaning, and devaluing the President of the United States and his policies – or – praying for him and loving him despite what actions he takes?

Do you hate the leaders whom we have been told are our enemies or whom we have been told are working against us- or- are you ignoring these voices and choosing to love our enemies the way Jesus Christ loved his enemies.

Do you find yourself getting angry with other people or people groups when you listen to right-wing or left-wing talk radio, when you watch news programs, and when you read the newspaper – or – are you tuning out and learning how to mercifully and gracefully love all people and all people groups despite their situation or circumstance?

Have your allegiance and identity become so closely aligned with the values of our country that you believe it is appropriate to kill people when they are deemed an "enemy" – or – are you on your knees seeking to better align yourself with the love and peace of Jesus toward friends and enemies alike?

Do your actions, when standing for a position on an issue (that you also happen to believe is the position of God), make you hurt, minimize, and wound individuals and people groups – or – do they heal, lift up, mend, and restore individuals and people groups in the loving, graceful, and merciful love of Christ?

Are your words and attitude toward others divisive, angry, hostile, demeaning, and devaluing when you disagree with their position or the way in which they live their lives – or – are your words and attitude always full of life, love, kindness, encouragement, and the building up of others?

We are just scratching the surface with these questions.

How does experiencing the all-consuming, enveloping, and overwhelming love of God change every part of our lives?

I pray it is changing us *in every way*.
And so much that it pours out of everything we do at all times.

Let the world only know us for our all-consuming, enveloping, and overwhelming love.
Nothing less.

_____

Jesus is calling us out of the large spectator crowd and along the narrow pathway with him.

He wants us to surrender every ounce of our lives to follow him and his way.

He wants us to walk away from a life that is easy.
He wants us to walk away from a life that is predictable.
He wants us to walk away from a life that is comfortable.

He wants us to enter into a life of risk.
He wants us to be willing to suffer pain and alienation.
He wants us to be willing to die.

For love.

Jesus expects everything from us.

And he is asking us to not just receive God's all-consuming, enveloping, and overwhelming love, but to also be willing to surrender our lives in order to give it away.

That is the place where sacrifice is needed.

And it begins today for those who want to be radical disciples, so that you will be ready in times of difficulty and hardship.

Let us be a people who are not stressed, anxious, or worried in our present lives or at the first sign of turmoil, but rather let us be a people who put our entire faith and hope in a God who takes care of His children.

Let us be a people who do not let the light of righteousness burn out in our present lives or as the world continues to grow darker around us, but rather let us be a people with a renewed sense that we are to have a unified purpose together extending the righteousness of God in the present, even as things become increasingly complex and chaotic.

Let us be a people who are not just announcing a watered-down Good News message with our lips presently or becoming even more silent in the face of opposition, but rather let us be a people who understand fully and unequivocally the life-changing, world-altering reality of the Good News of the kingdom and let us be a people who announce it to the world with our words, our lives, and our all.

Let us be a people who do not run from Jesus in the face of hostility and persecution, but rather let us be a courageous people who exist for a purpose in the way we love, encourage, serve, share a meal, embrace, and give all we have to our friends, enemies, and especially to others who are losing hope.

Let us be a people who are not easily swayed by propaganda, talking heads, political leaders, or any other thing that could lead us astray presently or as times become increasingly uncertain, but rather let us be a people resolved to know Jesus so intimately, his kingdom so thoroughly, his voice so specifically, that we could never be misguided.

And let us be a people who are not sucked into the national news headlines, the talk-show venom, the political mudslinging, the divisive rhetoric, and the cultural instigation presently or in times when it will be easier to blame and hate others, but rather let us be a people so overwhelmed and full of the love of God that we would rather give our lives than not give that love away.

So come ye people of "End Times" curiosity!
So come ye people of "End Times" zealousness!
So come ye people of "End Times" cynicism!
So come ye people of "End Times" indifference!

Let us unite as one behind Jesus Christ for the most important purpose this world has ever witnessed in history!

For the Good News of the kingdom will be preached throughout the whole world as a testimony to all the nations... AND THEN THE END WILL COME!

———

A LITTLE EXTRA!

While writing this book there was, no doubt, a backdrop that served to shape what I wrote.

It is a different perspective than what most Christians hear from week to week in mainline Christian churches.

That doesn't make this perspective wrong or misinformed. In fact, I believe it happens to be a perspective that Christianity lost as many pagan or secular ideas began to influence mainstream Christian thought.

It is a different perspective on our present identity and purpose as Christians, but also a different perspective on the hope we have for the future.

There are many Christians who also share this perspective, but being that most of you may have never heard it before… I would like to share it with you. It is just a brief and incomplete summary... but it will at least begin to paint a picture that you can see.

All I ask is that you...

Chew on it.

Pray over it.

And consider the possibilities.

But as I mentioned at the outset of the book, despite what differences we might have in perspective... the most important thing remains – *we must come together as one, united behind Jesus Christ for the most important declaration and demonstration in history... the Good News of the kingdom throughout the world.*

Peace and love, friends.

_____

I was talking to a friend who said that he did not want me to think poorly of him for his lack of excitement about going to heaven one day.

Of course he immediately got my full attention.

He said that from his perspective there is so much beauty in this world that he has not seen or experienced that the prospect of dying and "going to heaven for eternity" by comparison seemed like a huge let down.

The good news is that I didn't think poorly of my friend for his sentiments.

In fact, I appreciated his candor and honesty.

He is not wrong or bad for having deep, unfulfilled longings to explore, discover, and participate in the richness and fullness of God's good and amazing creation.

In many ways, I have the same unfulfilled longings.

I find myself thinking about how vast and diverse the earth is and how I long to see so much more of it than I will ever be able to in my lifetime and something within me just aches.

It is as if there is so much more to life on this earth than merely existing here for just a blink of the eye.

All of this led me to ask so many questions.

What if our longings are not wrong or misplaced?

What if God's good creation isn't a science experiment only to be discarded when the trial is over?

What if the Biblical narrative paints a very different picture of our future hope than the one many Christians have come to believe and understand?

What if God created all of this to be lived and experienced in its full glory...rather than lived in temporarily during which time it is marred and ruined by sin and death?

What if God's redemptive plan...God's victory and accomplishment in defeating sin and death through the resurrection of Jesus Christ... means something, not just for humanity, but for the entire created order that has suffered the consequences of sin and death?

Questions and possibilities such as these are exciting to consider and contemplate.

At one time, like much of mainstream Christianity, I believed heartily and steadfastly that the ultimate goal of the Christian was to join God in a disembodied, spiritual heaven for eternity when we die.

That belief was coupled with the notion that the current heaven and earth would be completely destroyed.

Through significant study and prayer, I no longer have that belief.

The hope that we have, as Christians, is not in a disembodied heaven, and God will not completely destroy His good creation.

In fact, the Biblical narrative paints such a convincing and compelling argument otherwise; I am surprised that we have missed it for so long.

I am convinced that the majority of you who are reading this believe in a disembodied future existence in heaven that will last for eternity… and you very well may be wondering how anyone, such as myself, who claims to be a Christian can believe anything differently.

I completely understand.

I have been on that page for 98% of my life, because the pervasive understanding and instruction within our churches, in regards to our hope in the future, has been exactly what I described above.

So why would anyone of us think otherwise, right?

My intention is not to wrestle you into submission or coerce you to change what you believe as much as I want to paint a different picture and offer, in my humble opinion, a more cohesive understanding of the hope we have for our future based upon an honest look at the Scriptures.

I believe that understanding this hope is of the utmost importance – *for what we believe about our future influences and informs our identity and purpose presently.*

The first place we must begin is with our understanding of the phrase: *kingdom of heaven*.

This is a phrase in which there has been serious misunderstanding. We have erroneously understood it as a disembodied future existence and destination for Christians rather than a present reality to be experienced and lived out in the hearts and lives of Christians, fully culminating when God establishes his kingdom on a renewed and restored earth.

If you look closely at the Gospels, you will notice that the author of Matthew uses the phrase *kingdom of heaven* instead of the phrase *kingdom of God* like the other Gospel authors. The author of Matthew used the word *heaven* instead of *God* because his letter was written to a Jewish audience, while the other Gospels were written primarily to Gentiles, or those who were not regarded as Jewish.

As you may know, practicing Jews do not write or utter the name of God, for they hold His name in holy reverence. Therefore, the author replaced the name of God, Yahweh, with the word *heaven*. Despite this one word being changed, the phrase kingdom of heaven was used to convey the same exact idea as the kingdom of God in the other Gospels.

So let's look further at this phrase *kingdom of heaven*, or *kingdom of God*, that is mentioned in the Gospels around 120 times and is regarded by Jesus as His primary message, the *Good News*, He came to announce.

The word *kingdom* is taken from the Greek word *basilea*, which means *reign or rule*. What we are dealing with in the Gospels, in essence, is the *reign of God* or the *reign of heaven*.

And this helps us take our first step.

As you may surmise, the *reign of heaven*, or the *reign of God*, isn't so much a place or location, as much as it is something that is happening.

147

It is something that is occurring.

The *reign of God* is a present reality.

And when God's reign is welcomed into a life... it is a present way of being.

We embody the *kingdom of God.*

It is akin to saying: *this is what life looks like when God reigns in and through our lives.*

It is, quite literally, the present reality of God's rule and reign in our hearts and it is actively moving among us.

This is backed up in the Gospel of Luke when Jesus said:

Nor will people say, Look! Here [it is]! Or, see [it is] there! For behold, the kingdom of God is within you [in your hearts] and among you [surrounding you].[28]

When Jesus used the phrase *kingdom of heaven*, or *kingdom of God*, it wasn't being used to describe a disembodied future destination for Christians. The phrase was being used to describe the present reality of God's reign breaking into our hearts, minds, and souls.

Think about the parables of Jesus.

Nearly every one of them began with him describing what the *kingdom of heaven* is like.

Jesus wasn't describing what heaven would be like one day.

He was describing what the reign of God is like right now on earth.

The parable of the sower is about the seed of God's reign being sown presently in the lives of people on earth.

The parable of the hidden treasure is about the treasure of God's reign being sought after presently in order to find the great riches of God on earth.

The parable of the pearl is about the pearl of God's reign that one is giving all of his earthly treasure to attain.

The parable of the farmer and the seed is about the seed of God's reign being sown presently and it growing on earth by God's power.

The parable of the mustard seed is about how the smallest seed of God's reign is taking root on earth and growing wildly and invasively throughout the entire earth.

The parable of the yeast is about how a small portion of God's reign is working into the dough of the earth and how it is growing and expanding.

The parable of the lost sheep is about how God's reign is presently seeking and searching after the lost person.

The parable of the lost coin is about how God's reign is presently seeking to find a person who has been lost and then celebrating when he is found.

There are more parables.

The Good Samaritan.
The Ten Virgins.
The Two Debtors.
The Unjust Judge.

And so on.

And in each and every instance Jesus is describing the present reality of the in-breaking *reign of God/reign of heaven* on earth.

Again, it is what our present reality looks like when God's reign breaks forth on earth…and this is what our lives look like when we presently welcome God's reign into our lives.

The implications of this are utterly profound.

God's reign on earth has been initiated.

God's reign has come close and is breaking into our lives in power.

The veil that separates the dimension of God and our dimension has been pierced and God's reign and rule is flooding the earth.

God's reign is invading earth presently through our lives and is rushing with full force until his reign is fully and completely manifested on earth.

The union of heaven and earth is continuing until it reaches its full consummation.

Your kingdom come your will be done on earth as it is in heaven.

The two are gloriously becoming one as God's reign fills the cosmos.

The *kingdom of heaven* is not a future destination for a disembodied soul. The *kingdom of heaven* is the present in-breaking of God's reign on earth, pouring in until it reaches its full measure at his triumphant return.

Heaven and earth will then be together as one again.

From the words of the prophets in the Old Testament leading up to and culminating in the teachings of Jesus and then passed along through the writings to the early Church, there is a sense that God isn't giving up on the creation that was called "good" from the very beginning.

In fact, there is very clear scriptural evidence that God has always had every intention of renewing and restoring the entire created order, rather than destroying it.

This is a strong assertion, being that it contradicts the teaching and understanding of many Churches that teach how God will one day destroy the heavens and the earth...and then take Christians away to a spiritual heaven to live for eternity.

But as we look through the Biblical narrative: we find all of creation suffering under the weight of death and decay.[29]

We find all of creation subjected to frustration. We find all of creation groaning for liberation from the curse under which it is has been placed.[30]

It is a physical creation.

It is a tangible creation.

It is a touchable creation.

It is a physical, tangible, touchable creation that wants to be liberated, freed, released from bondage.

It is a creation that is enslaved...and longs to be as it once was... not destroyed, not annihilated, not discarded, and not thrown into the trash bin of history. It is a creation that yearns to be saved, renewed, and restored.

And it is not just the creation in which we live and which surrounds us that will be completely renewed and restored!

We long for liberation from death and decay as well.[31]

Presently we have and enjoy the first fruits of the Holy Spirit given to us by God, which gives us a foretaste of the blissful things to come, but we also groan inwardly as we wait for the redemption of our bodies, which will reveal our adoption, or our manifestation as God's sons and daughters.

This surprising discovery, which stands in contrast to the belief that God will one day destroy the heavens and the earth, is a beautiful synergy of God's restorative work through Jesus Christ, not just for humanity, but also for the entire created order.

For God so loved the world (*kosmos – the entire created order*) that He sent His Son.[32]

But despite the fact that Paul wrote about how creation will be set free from its bondage to decay and corruption.

Despite the fact that Paul wrote about how heaven and earth will be brought together under Christ.[33]

Despite the fact that Jesus talked to the disciples about the renewal of all things.[34]

And despite the fact that Peter stated that God will restore everything.[35]

There are still a couple of misunderstood verses that have led us to the belief that the earth will one day be destroyed and that our future hope is a disembodied, spiritual heaven.

...and the material elements of the universe will flare and melt with fire. But we look for new heavens and a new earth according to His promise, in which righteousness (uprightness, freedom from sin, and right standing with God) is to abide. 2 Peter 3: 12-13

Then I saw a new sky (heaven) and a new earth, for the former sky and the former earth had passed away, and there no longer existed any sea. Revelation 21: 1

At first glance, these verses seemingly contradict the very position I have proposed – *that God is in the process of renewing and restoring all of creation.*

But the key to unlocking these verses, and having a better and more comprehensive understanding of what the text is really saying, lies with the word *new.*

As we look at the original Greek language we find something very interesting.

There are two words that can be used to describe something as *new.*

The first word is *neo* and is used to describe something that is *new in time.*

For example, a house that is newly restored to its original condition could never be *neo* because it is not *new in time.*

When the house was first built it was *neo*, but being that it is now something old (*archaios*) being renewed or restored, it can ever be described as *neo* again.

Neo is not the word used in the passages above from 2 Peter or Revelation.

The word that is used to describe the new heavens and the new earth in those passages is the word *kainos.*

Kainos also means *new*, but it is describing something that is *qualitatively new or renewed.*

Interestingly enough, it is the word *kainos* that Paul uses to describe the Christian, as a *new* (*kainos*) creation.

The individual Christian has not been vaporized into non-existence and then newly created, rather the *old* (*archaios*) has passed away, and the *new* (*kainos*) has come.[36]

Therefore, the passages are not alluding to a heaven and earth that are destroyed and then replaced by a heaven and earth that are newly created.

They are both speaking of the current heaven and earth passing from one condition to another (*parachomai*), more like being refined by the refiner's fire, and then being *qualitatively renewed* (*kainos*) to their full glory, which is beyond anything that we can comprehend.

Behold, I am making all things new (kainos)…

The final destination for God's people is not "going up" to God in heaven, while the earth and sky are destroyed.

Rather, the hope we have for our future is in a *renewed world and renewed cosmos* in which God's dwelling place is among his people.

If that doesn't get you excited about the possibilities in our future I don't know what will.

That is why throughout the main portion of this book I always put the phrase *End Times* in quotation marks.

Because many people believe that the phrase "End Times" refers to the time preceding the "End of the World."

However, there are others, including me, who do not believe the "End Times" has anything at all to do with the "End of the World," but rather the "End of the Age."

So who is right?

Well, there is a good reason why so many believe that the "End Times" refers to the "End of the World." And the easiest explanation is the King James translation.

For example, take the Matthew 24 passage that we discussed throughout the first half of this book.

The King James Version reads like this:

Tell us, when shall these things be? And what shall be the sign of thy coming, and of the end of the world?[87]

This translation clearly and unambiguously conveys that the disciples wanted to know what the sign of Christ's return would be before the "end of the world."

Right?

And because of the King James translation, many beliefs and theologies have been shaped and formed around the idea that the world will "come to an end."

However, there is another perspective that believes the original Greek language was not translated accurately and instead of the passage reading as the "end of the world," it should have read as "the end of the age."

The difference here is monumental.

Here is how other versions of the same passage read:

When will this happen, and what will be the sign of your coming and of the end of the age?[88]

Tell us, when will this take place, and what will be the sign of Your coming and of the end (the completion, the consummation) of the age?[89]

Tell us, when will these things happen, and what will be the sign of Your coming, and of the end of the age?[40]

Tell us, when will these things be, and what will be the sign of your coming and of the close of the age?[41]

The difference between the King James and the other versions raise two big questions.

What exactly is the Greek word or phrase that was translated as "world" or "age?"

What does that particular Greek word or phrase really mean?

Well, the Greek word under investigation here is *Aiōn*.

The meaning of *Aiōn* is *an age, a cycle of time.*

Jews understood an age this way: the age before the return of the Messiah and the establishment of his reign on earth – and – the age after the return of the Messiah and the establishment of his reign on earth.

And that is what was written.
And that is what was supposed to be conveyed.

In this order.

The Present Age.
The End of the Age.
The Age to Come.

Each of them with the focal point of the Messiah's return and establishment of his kingdom on earth.

Nowhere was it ever meant to convey the "end of the world."

Strong's Greek Lexicon describes the Present Age (*Aiōn*) this way:

The time before the appointed return or truly Messianic advent of Christ. The period of instability, weakness, impiety, wickedness, calamity, misery.

And then describes the Age to Come (*Aiōn*) this way:

The age after the return of Christ in majesty. The period of the consummate establishment of the divine kingdom and all its blessings.

There is so much more that could be said about this word, because it has also been mistranslated as *forever* and *eternity*, but for the sake of this discussion – the Greek word *Aiōn* does not mean world. It means age, or cycle of time.

So let's put this all together so far.

The kingdom of God (God's reign) has been initiated in the Present Age in hearts and minds of those who believe.

And in the Present Age we continue to extend the Good News of God's reign, or kingdom, as if we were sowing the seeds in the hearts and minds of other people, so as to make preparations on earth for the coming Messiah.

When the Messiah returns, the End of the Age will come.

Jesus will hand over the kingdom to God the Father after he has destroyed all dominion, authority, and power.[42]

God's reign and glory will flood the earth as He makes His dwelling place among mankind and the consummation of heaven and earth will commence the Age to Come in a newly restored and refined earth.[43]

This is a huge step we have taken together, but it raises at least two questions.

What about the Rapture?

What about our bodies (Will we be spirits or will we have bodies)?

_____

Let's quickly answer the Rapture question.

The Rapture is explained as a moment that will take place in the twinkling of an eye in which Christians will vanish from the earth and be taken to heaven with Christ.

That is basically it in a nutshell.

There may be a little variation among people, but that is the essence.

There are several problems with the idea of the Rapture.

It is a modern idea based thinly on two verses in 1 Corinthians 15: 51-52 and 1 Thessalonians 4:17, respectively:

Listen, I tell you a mystery: We will not all sleep, but we will all be changed— in a flash, in the twinkling of an eye, at the last trumpet. For the trumpet will sound, the dead will be raised imperishable, and we will be changed.

After that, we who are still alive and are left will be caught up together with them in the clouds to meet the Lord in the air. And so we will be with the Lord forever.

I will deal with the Corinthian passage shortly when I discuss the resurrection and our resurrection bodies.

So let's first turn our attention to the passage in 1 Thessalonians.

There are many assumptions that have been made about this verse.

It is assumed that we will instantly vanish into spiritual beings, that we will meet Jesus in the sky, and that he will take us away with him to heaven.

Based upon the foundation we built earlier, I concluded that this world isn't a place from where we are trying to escape.

Rather, it is a place we are preparing so that we may accompany and welcome back the Lord as he returns for the Wedding Feast.

Remember the parable about the Ten Virgins?

When they went out to meet the Groom, he did not turn around and take them back to the place from which he came.

No!

The virgins went out to greet him and then led the wedding processional back to the place that had been prepared for the Wedding Feast celebration.

This symmetry here is just exquisite.

But to take the Rapture theology a step further.

It is an invention that was not a part of the early Church.

In fact, the idea of the Rapture is a relatively new idea in Christendom, making its first public appearance in the early 1800's. It was not an idea proposed by Christ or carried on throughout the early Church, because that belief simply did not exist.

I do not want to discount the idea that we will be caught up to meet the Lord in the air at some point, but I just don't happen to believe that he is taking us away to a spiritual heaven.

Instead, we will accompany him back so that he may destroy all dominion, authority, and power structures on earth, and then hand over the kingdom to God the Father, who will have made his dwelling place among us.

_____

Let's now turn our attention to the other question about our future bodies, which Scriptures describes as the resurrection body.

Again, what we believe about our end significantly influences our present.

This isn't just true for the topic at hand; it is also true in our everyday experiences.

For instance, good companies have a vision and goals that orient their daily work toward those ends. And as a result, workers understand their work presently through the lens of where the company ultimately wants to be.

This principle is important for our current discussion.

If the ultimate goal of one's life is to go to a disembodied spiritual heaven with God for eternity... then not only will one's life activities (and the Church's activities) be oriented around that end... but how one reads Scripture will be oriented around and influenced by that end as well.

But, if our future hope is actually different than a disembodied spiritual heaven for eternity, and I believe it is, then it will not only influence our understanding of our present identity and purpose in the world, it will also help us better understand Scripture as it relates to that end.

I cannot underscore how important this point is for us to understand.

Let's look at the end (the hope that we have for our future), so we may better understand some seemingly confusing scriptures in light of it:

Then I heard a mighty voice from the throne and I perceived its distinct words, saying, See! The abode of God is with men, and He will live (encamp, tent) among them; and they shall be His people, and God shall personally be with them and be their God.

God will wipe away every tear from their eyes; and death shall be no more, neither shall there be anguish (sorrow and mourning) nor grief nor pain any more, for the old conditions and the former order of things have passed away.[44]

There should not be any question that the consummation (the fulfillment, the bringing together) of our future hope looks like this: *God living among us in a renewed and restored creation where the former order of things have passed away and where there will be no more death, anguish, sorrow, or mourning.*

Since this is the case, it only makes logical sense that the hope we have for our future does not involve us as disembodied spirits floating around, but rather as people who are clothed in new bodies, fully integrated spiritual bodies, that will feel, touch, sense, experience, taste, smell, hear, sing, and talk.

Having this understanding helps us unlock another commonly misunderstood passage in which Paul is writing to clear up significant misunderstanding by the Corinthians of, not just the physical resurrection of Jesus, but also of the future physical resurrection of believers.

His contention is that there is absolutely no point of putting his life on the line if Christ has not been raised from the dead:

What do I gain if, merely from a human point of view, I fought wild beasts at Ephesus...if the dead are not raised at all.[45]

But, since Christ (the first fruits) has been raised to resurrection life, he is confident that those who belong to Christ will also experience the same bodily resurrection – for if the dead are not raised then Christ has not been raised.

Let me be clear...Paul is making the emphatic point that those who belong to Christ presently are guaranteed a bodily resurrection at some point after they die.

And at this point in Paul's letter, he begins to get even more frustrated at the Corinthian's lack of understanding of the bodily resurrection, so he begins to get incredibly specific in his argument with imagery that he hopes they will understand.

And this is where undue confusion for the average Christian has occurred.

Paul says, that in the same way a seed must die when planted in order to then spring up as a different kind of body, so too the human body dies but will rise in another kind of body.

So it is with the resurrection of the dead:

[The body] that is sown is perishable and decays, but [the body] that is resurrected is imperishable [immune to decay, immortal].

It is sown in dishonor and humiliation; it is raised in honor and glory.

It is sown in infirmity and weakness; it is resurrected in strength and endued power.

It is sown a natural (physical) body; it is raised a supernatural (a spiritual) body.

[As surely as] there is a physical body, there is also a spiritual body.[46]

Had Paul wanted to say that a person becomes a spirit, he may have used a noun such as spirit (*pneuma*).

But he doesn't.

He used the word body (*soma*) and then qualified it with the adjective spiritual (*pneumatikos*), which implies that Paul's understanding of a resurrection body was a fully realized and fully integrated physical and spiritual body that is imperishable, honorable, glorious, strong, powerful, and supernatural.

To be sure that this is the case, Paul never once used the adjective *pneumatikos* to describe anything as a disembodied spirit.

In fact, every time that the word *pneumatikos* was used by Paul in the New Testament, it was to convey the mark of the Holy Spirit on an object.

Oddly enough, Paul described those of us who presently have the Holy Spirit as being *pneumatikos* (spiritual), and we are certainly not disembodied spirits right now!

The greatest evidence of new (*kainos*) creation and the renewal of all things, is the resurrection of Jesus Christ.

For in this singular event the physical body of Jesus, which was once dead, came back as resurrected life – not as an apparition or bodiless spirit but as fully realized, supernatural, spiritual body.

In the resurrected Christ we find the most perfectly integrated and the most fully realized Spirit (*pneuma*) and body (*soma*).

That is the hope we have for the future, a spiritual (*pneumatikos*) body (*soma*).

Christ had a resurrection body of supernatural form that was tangible and touchable, for even Thomas the doubter was able to see and touch!

One day, that which we have been given a foretaste of presently (a portion of the Spirit)…will be the full measure.

And while we inwardly have the profound joy of experiencing what it is to be *pneumatikos*, we groan inwardly and long for the day when our bodies will be *pneumatikos*, as well.

_____

The primary dilemma in front of many Christians, maybe you, is this: *I have always been taught that when a person dies he or she goes to heaven. Now you are telling me that a disembodied, spiritual heaven is not the end. I am not sure that is something I can believe.*

I can assure you that there was a day many years ago when I said the same thing.

It doesn't make you a bad person for vocalizing your internal conflict; in fact, it is quite normal and healthy.

It means that you are, at a minimum, wrestling with it rather than putting up your dukes, acting like you already know everything there is to know about the hope we have for our future, and then resisting to listen and giving up the opportunity to learn something new.

Listening and dialogue are so important.

It is obviously the place where we may learn something new, but it is also the place where we walk alongside each other in love and grace while uncovering more truth.

My perspective on heaven is not some new idea that I just decided to throw out there.

I have wrestled and prayed over it the last six years.

I have studied, researched, prayed, and left no stone unturned in the process.

When I wrote my book *Unearthed* in 2010, I so badly wanted to include all of this information about heaven in it to synthesize and solidify my position on the Kingdom of God, but realized even at that time that I was not ready to write about it or discuss it.

But not too long after that I felt something opening up about the topic of heaven and the renewal of all things.

For every way my writing felt blocked or forced a couple of years ago on this topic, it was now coming to me at lightning speed.

It was time for people to hear a different perspective.

It was time to introduce people to a more complete understanding of the hope Christians have.

It was time to challenge the culturally-developed idea of heaven that the Church has adopted.

It was time to reconnect with the belief and understanding that Judaism, Jesus, and the Early Church had concerning God's redemptive plan for all of His good creation.

Let me be clear here – what I have written to this point has NOT been a discussion of what happens to a person as soon as he or she dies or where that person goes.

I have focused only on the End of the Age and the return of Christ.

So while it is certainly worth discussing what happens immediately after a person dies, that is not my interest here. There are other books, blogs, and writings that discuss that topic.

Rather, what I have been describing is God's plan of redemption and what the hope we have for the future will look like when Christ returns.

Just because there may be a waiting place for those who have died, doesn't mean that is where it all ends.

My point has been that Scripture offers a surprising twist that is different than what many of us have been taught. And, I believe the beginning of that surprise is simply and straightforwardly with the resurrection of Jesus Christ.

So, what was the point of the resurrection of Jesus Christ?

The simple answer – *for God to demonstrate decisively that sin and death does not have the final victory over that which God created as good at the very beginning.*

In fact, the resurrection declares that God wins, and through Jesus, there is more where that came from!

Death will no longer have a sting!

What was evidenced in Jesus, the resurrection, is promised to those who put their hope in Him – and that is victory over death.

So the logical question at this point is – *what does sin and death have an effect on?*

That's right...physical things.

Think about it... if death's sting has been enacted upon a physical body, does not the defeat of death through resurrection mean that this body shall live?

Again, what would be the point of a physical resurrection evidenced in Christ if our own future is spirit or ghost-like?

Even more, since a bodily resurrection demonstrates God's victory over sin and death, and the promise that death will no longer have a sting on God's people, it can only mean that death will no longer have a stranglehold on that which God created as good from the very beginning.

The resurrection screams, "EVERYTHING IS WORTH SAVING!"

It simply would not make any logical sense for God to create something as "good" only to discard it when the oppositional forces of evil disrupt or mar it.

For the sake of logic alone, not even considering Church history or scripture, I can deductively conclude that the redemptive plan of God has never been to destroy the creation and whisk people off to a disembodied, spiritual heaven for eternity.

_____

I have been offering glimpses from scripture of what God's true intention has always been and what it continues to be – *not taking people away to a disembodied heaven for eternity, but rather working to redeem, renew, and restore all of His good creation through the defeat of sin and death as evidenced and initiated in the resurrection of Jesus Christ.*

In Jesus, the bringing together of heaven and earth has been launched in the Present Age and we look forward to the Age to Come, in which the full consummation of heaven and earth will be complete with God making His dwelling place among us in a renewed and restored earth.

We didn't arrive in this place by accident.

The Scriptures from Genesis forward evidence a God who has been working painstakingly to remedy, mend, and heal that which was fractured and broken from the very beginning – not just people, but all things.

The central purpose, the grand narrative, the over-arching

achievement of God is to: bring heaven and earth back together as one.

Jesus said to them, Truly I say to you, in the new age [the Messianic rebirth of the world], when the Son of Man shall sit down on the throne of His glory, you who have [become My disciples, sided with My party and] followed Me will also sit on twelve thrones and judge the twelve tribes of Israel. Matthew 19: 28 AMP

So repent (change your mind and purpose); turn around and return [to God], that your sins may be erased (blotted out, wiped clean), that times of refreshing (of recovering from the effects of heat, of reviving with fresh air) may come from the presence of the Lord; And that He may send [to you] the Christ (the Messiah), Who before was designated and appointed for you—even Jesus, Whom heaven must receive [and retain] until the time for the complete restoration of all that God spoke by the mouth of all His holy prophets for ages past [from the most ancient time in the memory of man]. Acts 3: 19-21 AMP

For [even the whole] creation (all nature) waits expectantly and longs earnestly for God's sons to be made known [waits for the revealing, the disclosing of their sonship]. For the creation (nature) was subjected to frailty (to futility, condemned to frustration), not because of some intentional fault on its part, but by the will of Him Who so subjected it—[yet] with the hope that nature (creation) itself will be set free from its bondage to decay and corruption [and gain an entrance] into the glorious freedom of God's children. We know that the whole creation [of irrational creatures] has been moaning together in the pains of labor until now. And not only the creation, but we ourselves too, who have and enjoy the firstfruits of the [Holy] Spirit [a foretaste of the blissful things to come] groan inwardly as we wait for the redemption of our bodies [from sensuality and the grave, which will reveal] our adoption (our manifestation as God's sons). Romans 8: 19-23 AMP

In Him we have redemption (deliverance and salvation) through His blood, the remission (forgiveness) of our offenses (shortcomings and trespasses), in accordance with the riches and the generosity of His gracious favor, Which He lavished upon us in every kind of wisdom and understanding (practical insight and prudence), Making known to us the mystery (secret) of His will (of His plan, of His purpose). [And it is this:] In accordance with His good pleasure (His merciful intention) which He had previously purposed and set forth in Him, [He planned] for the maturity of the times and the climax of the ages to unify all things and head them up and consummate them in Christ, [both] things in heaven and things on the earth. Ephesians 1: 7-10 AMP

For it was in Him that all things were created, in heaven and on earth, things seen and things unseen, whether thrones, dominions, rulers, or authorities; all things were created and exist through Him [by His service, intervention] and in and for Him. And He Himself existed before all things, and in Him all things consist (cohere, are held together). He also is the Head of [His] body, the Church; seeing He is the Beginning, the Firstborn from among the dead, so that He alone in everything and in every respect might occupy the chief place [stand first and be preeminent]. For it has pleased [the Father] that all the divine fullness (the sum total of the divine perfection, powers, and attributes) should dwell in Him permanently. And God purposed that through (by the service, the intervention of) Him [the Son] all things should be completely reconciled back to Himself, whether on earth or in heaven, as through Him, [the Father] made peace by means of the blood of His cross. Colossians 1: 16-20 AMP

It is obvious that the weight and trajectory of the Scriptures come together in the victory and accomplishment of Jesus Christ through His death on the cross and resurrection to new life...and describe the objects of this salvific activity as a complete reconciliation and restoration of all things in the Age to Come – our bodies, the creation, everything, and all things in heaven and earth.

For all that had gone wrong in the garden, it is the gardener who fixes it and restores it.

In every way our paths have been crooked, there will be a day when they are all made straight.

In every way God intended for us to be helpers and caretakers of His good creation, His original intention will be realized in the new heaven and new earth.

In every way nature has suffered the curse, producing thorn and thistle, and animals have had enmity toward man and one another, there will be a time when wine will flow from mountains and the lion will lie with the lamb in peace.

In every way we have been told, or have come to believe, that we are of little value or significance, we will fully and finally realize the profound value we have in God's eyes since the creation of the world.

In every way relationships were fractured and broken because of our rebellion against God and our distrust and hatred of one another, there will be perfect harmony, unity, and community one with another and all with God.

In every way we have longed for peace and justice, and held out hope that there would be a better day, we will one day beat our swords into plowshares and our spears into pruning hooks, never again lifting a sword against another, nor learning of war any more, for the love of God will fill the cosmos.

In every way nation has risen against nation and kingdom against kingdom, the fullness and completeness of God's glory and peace throughout the land will reveal the cultural beauty and uniqueness of every nation as they are healed and celebrated.

In every way rulers have crushed, oppressed, and killed those whom they have subjugated, we will one day experience the loving, merciful, and victorious leadership of Jesus and those who rule with Him.

In every way we have split and divided over race, social status, and economic achievement, dishonoring God in the process, the nations will one day gather united in our diversity and worship God as one.

In every way our bodies have given out, been debilitated or handicapped, and suffered the crushing weight of disease and death, we will one day have incorruptible, resurrection bodies that will do things we could never imagine.

And in every way we have longed for and anticipated eating and drinking anew with Christ and one another in the fully realized and consummated Kingdom of God, we will one day sing praises, give thanks, break bread, and celebrate the salvation and the power and the Kingdom of our God, and the power of His Messiah.

Amen!

REFERENCES

1. Matthew 6: 34
2. Matthew 6: 25
3. Luke 21: 9
4. John 14: 1
5. Luke 12: 32
6. Matthew 28: 20
7. Matthew 25: 1-13
8. Matthew 25: 14-30
9. Matthew 25: 31-46
10. Luke 4: 43
11. Acts 1: 3
12. Luke 8: 5-15
13. Matthew 13: 44
14. Matthew 13: 45
15. Matthew 13: 31-32
16. Matthew 13: 33
17. Matthew 13: 24-30
18. Matthew 13: 47-50
19. Luke 17: 21
20. Matthew 5: 10
21. Matthew 5: 11

22. Matthew 5: 44
23. John 15: 20
24. John 10: 27
25. Luke 14: 25-27
26. Luke 14: 33
27. John 14: 6
28. Luke 17: 20-21
29. Romans 8: 20-21
30. Romans 8: 22
31. Romans 8: 23
32. John 3: 16
33. Ephesians 1: 7-10
34. Matthew 19: 28
35. Acts 3: 17-21
36. 2 Corinthians 5: 17
37. Matthew 24: 3 KJV
38. Matthew 24: 3 NIV
39. Matthew 24: 3 AMP
40. Matthew 24: 3 NASB
41. Matthew 24: 3 ESV
42. 1 Corinthians 15: 23-24
43. Revelation 21: 1-5
44. Revelation 21: 3-4
45. 1 Corinthians 15: 32
46. 1 Corinthians 15: 34-45